Series/Number 07-082

SUMMATED RATING SCALE CONSTRUCTION
An Introduction

PAUL E. SPECTOR
University of South Florida

SAGE PUBLICATIONS
The International Professional Publishers
Newbury Park   London   New Delhi

For information address:

 SAGE Publications, Inc.
2455 Teller Road
Newbury Park, California 91320

SAGE Publications Ltd.
6 Bonhill Street
London EC2A 4PU
United Kingdom

SAGE Publications India Pvt. Ltd.
M-32 Market
Greater Kailash I
New Delhi 110 048 India

Printed in the United States of America

Library of Congress Cataloging-in-Publication Data

Spector, Paul E.
    Summated rating scale construction : an introduction / Paul E. Spector.
        p. cm. — (Sage university papers series. Quantitative applications in the social sciences, no. 82)
    Includes bibliographical references.
    ISBN 0-8039-4341-5
    1. Scaling (Social sciences)   I. Title   II. Series.
H61.27.S66   1992
300'.72 — dc20   91-36161

FIRST PRINTING, 1992

Sage Production Editor: Astrid Virding

When citing a university paper, please use the proper form. Remember to cite the current Sage University Paper series title and include the paper number. One of the following formats can be adapted (depending on the style manual used):

(1) SPECTOR, P. E. (1992) Summated Rating Scale Construction: An Introduction. Sage University Paper Series on Quantitative Applications in the Social Sciences, 07-082. Newbury Park, CA: Sage.

OR

(2) Spector, P. E. (1992) *Summated Rating Scale Construction: An Introduction.* (Sage University Paper series on Quantitative Applications in the Social Sciences, series no. 07-082). Newbury Park, CA: Sage.

CONTENTS

SERIES EDITOR'S INTRODUCTION

Across the social sciences, summated rating scales are much in use. A political scientist may pose several items to survey respondents about their "trust in government," adding up scores to form an index for each. A sociologist might ask a sample of workers to evaluate their "subjective social class" in a battery of questions, summing responses into one measure. Or else a psychologist, as in the case of Dr. Spector, could construct a Work Locus of Control Scale, based on numerous agree-disagree Likert-type items. In each example, the goal is development of an individual rating on some attitude, value, or opinion.

The task of constructing good summated rating scales is seldom easy. Furthermore, in many graduate training programs, there is not enough learned instruction in *how* to construct such scales. Thus, for the underseasoned graduate student who has to come up with one, as well as for the faculty member who needs a refresher, this monograph is invaluable. Spector gives us, clearly and carefully, the necessary steps to build these scales.

Take the example of the young political scientist studying political values, in particular that of "free speech." In the survey instrument, this student asks respondents simply to "agree" or "disagree" with the following item:

Communists have a right to speak just like the rest.

Is one item enough to measure our concept of free speech? "No," says Spector, as he begins his explanation. He examines not only why multiple items are necessary, but also the appropriate number of response categories and the preferred item wording. After that, he gives guidelines for sorting good items from bad, including item-remainder coefficients and Cronbach's alpha. Once the item analysis is complete, it is time for validation of the scale. Does it mean what it is supposed to mean? Multiple standards of validity, including dimensional validity

v

from factor analysis, are considered. Next comes the treatment of scale reliability and norms.

Throughout the presentation, Spector is sensitive to issues of theory. The empirical tests never prove a theoretical construct exists, but they may point to its existence. As he remarks in his conclusion, the "development of a scale is an ongoing process that really never ends."

—Michael S. Lewis-Beck
Series Editor

SUMMATED RATING SCALE CONSTRUCTION: An Introduction

PAUL E. SPECTOR
University of South Florida

1. INTRODUCTION

The summated rating scale is one of the most frequently used tools in the social sciences. Its invention is attributed to Rensis Likert (1932), who described this technique for the assessment of attitudes. These scales are widely used across the social sciences to measure not only attitudes, but opinions, personalities, and descriptions of people's lives and environments as well. Scales presently exist that measure emotional states (e.g., anger, anxiety, and depression), personal needs (e.g., achievement, autonomy, and power), personality (e.g., locus of control and introversion), and description of jobs (e.g., role ambiguity and workload). These are but a few of the hundreds of variables for which scales have been developed. For many variables several scales exist, some of which were created for specialized purposes.

There are four characteristics that make a scale a summated rating scale. First, a scale must contain multiple items. The use of *summated* in the name implies that multiple items will be combined or summed. Second, each individual item must measure something that has an underlying, quantitative measurement continuum. In other words, it measures a property of something that can vary quantitatively rather than qualitatively. An attitude, for example, can vary from being very favorable to being very unfavorable. Third, each item has no "right" answer, which makes the summated rating scale different from a multiple-choice test. Thus summated rating scales cannot be used to test for knowledge or ability. Finally, each item in a scale is a statement, and respondents are asked to give ratings about each statement. This involves asking subjects to indicate which of several response choices best reflects their response to the item. Most summated rating scales offer between four and seven response choices.

Table 1.1 contains the Work Locus of Control Scale (WLCS; Spector, 1988) as an example of a summated rating scale. The WLCS is a 16 item, 6 response choice, agreement scale. There are three things to note about the scale. First, at the top is the key containing the six response choices, ordered from greatest disagreement to greatest agreement. The greatest disagreement, *disagree very much,* is given the lowest value of 1. The greatest agreement, *agree very much,* is given the highest value of 6. Below the key are the statements or item stems for which respondents will indicate their level of agreement. To the right of each stem are all six possible responses. Respondents circle one response for each item.

The WLCS represents a popular format for a summated rating scale, but alternate variations also can be found. For example, respondents can be asked to write down the number representing their response to each item, rather than circling a number. Discussions to follow refer to all summated rating scales, regardless of the particular format options that are chosen.

The WLCS is a scale that was developed by the current author (Spector, 1988). Its development will serve as an example throughout this monograph, because it illustrates the steps involved in developing these scales. I certainly do not claim that this scale is in any way better, more carefully developed, or more construct valid than other scales. Rather, the strategy adopted for its development was typical of that used by scale developers.

The summated rating-scale format is often used for several reasons. First, it can produce scales that have good *psychometric* properties— that is, a well-developed summated rating scale can have good reliability and validity. Second, a summated rating scale is relatively cheap and easy to develop. The writing of items is straightforward, and the initial development of the scale requires only 100 to 200 subjects. Finally, a well-devised scale is usually quick and easy for respondents to complete and typically does not induce complaints from them.

Of course, there are also drawbacks. Perhaps the biggest limitation is that subjects must have a reasonably high level of literacy. Potential respondents who do not read well will certainly have difficulty completing these scales. Another is that some level of expertise and statistical sophistication is necessary to develop a good scale. However, I

TABLE 1.1

The Work Locus of Control Scale (WLCS)

The following questions concern your beliefs about jobs in general. They do not refer only to your present job.

1 = Disagree very much	4 = Agree slightly
2 = Disagree moderately	5 = Agree moderately
3 = Disagree slightly	6 = Agree very much

1. A job is what you make of it.   1 2 3 4 5 6
2. On most jobs, people can pretty much accomplish whatever they set out to accomplish.   1 2 3 4 5 6
3. If you know what you want out of a job, you can find a job that gives it to you.   1 2 3 4 5 6
4. If employees are unhappy with a decision made by their boss, they should do something about it.   1 2 3 4 5 6
5. Getting the job you want is mostly a matter of luck.   1 2 3 4 5 6
6. Making money is primarily a matter of good fortune.   1 2 3 4 5 6
7. Most people are capable of doing their jobs well if they make the effort.   1 2 3 4 5 6
8. In order to get a really good job, you need to have family members or friends in high places.   1 2 3 4 5 6
9. Promotions are usually a matter of good fortune.   1 2 3 4 5 6
10. When it comes to landing a really good job, who you know is more important than what you know.   1 2 3 4 5 6
11. Promotions are given to employees who perform well on the job.   1 2 3 4 5 6
12. To make a lot of money you have to know the right people.   1 2 3 4 5 6
13. It takes a lot of luck to be an outstanding employee on most jobs.   1 2 3 4 5 6
14. People who perform their jobs well generally get rewarded.   1 2 3 4 5 6
15. Most employees have more influence on their supervisors than they think they do.   1 2 3 4 5 6
16. The main difference between people who make a lot of money and people who make a little money is luck.   1 2 3 4 5 6

have seen undergraduates with a course or two in statistics and/or measurement devise good scales with some guidance. As with most things, it is not too difficult to develop a scale once you know how.

The goal of this monograph is to explain in detail how to develop a summated rating scale. The procedures described here are those typically followed in the development of most scales by individual researchers. Test development projects by major testing firms, such as

Educational Testing Service or the Psychological Corporation, are often more involved and utilize much larger samples of subjects. Their general approach, however, is much like the one described here.

All the steps necessary for scale construction will be covered in detail. Advice will be provided to avoid the pitfalls that doom a scale development effort. For someone developing a scale for the first time, this monograph alone is not sufficient as a guide to scale construction. Additional guidance from someone with experience in scale construction is recommended. At the very least, this person should review procedures, items, and the results of analyses conducted.

Why Use Multiple-Item Scales?

The development of a summated rating scale requires a considerable investment of time and effort. It also requires that respondents will be able to take several minutes to provide their ratings. A reasonable question is why go to all the bother? To determine someone's opinion, why not just ask them with a single, straightforward, yes-or-no question?

There are three good reasons why single yes-or-no questions are insufficient. They concern reliability, precision, and scope. Single items do not produce responses by people that are consistent over time. A person may answer "yes" today and "no" tomorrow. Thus single items are notoriously unreliable. They are also imprecise because they restrict measurement to only two levels. People can be placed into only two groups, with no way to distinguish among people in each group. Finally, many measured characteristics are broad in scope and not easily assessed with a single question. Some issues are complex, and several items will be necessary to assess them.

These problems are best illustrated with an example. A frequently studied domain is people's feeling about the government. To assess feelings, a single question could be asked, such as

Do you like the government? (Yes or No).

Unfortunately, all people who respond "yes" will not have the same strength of feeling. Some may love the government; others may only slightly like it. Likewise, some people responding "no" will hate the government, whereas others will merely dislike it. People in the middle who have ambivalent feelings will be forced to choose either yes or no and will be counted along with those with strong feelings. Thus there is inadequate precision for most purposes.

Unreliability or inconsistency in people's responses over time will be produced in several ways. First, the ambivalent people may be making essentially random responses to the question. Depending upon the day, the person's mood, and the weather, the ambivalents may answer either "yes" or "no." If an ambivalent person is asked the same question on different occasions, inconsistency would be observed. In fact, responding yes and no each 50% of the time would define ambivalence in a psychophysical sense.[1]

Unreliability also can be produced by respondents making mistakes in their responses. They may mean to respond "yes" and instead respond "no", they may misread the question (e.g., "I *dis*like the government"), or they may misunderstand the question. They may be uncertain about what the question means. Does "government" mean federal government, state government, local government, or all three? All these factors introduce errors that lead to unreliability.

The final difficulty is that people's feelings may not be this simple. They may like certain aspects of government and not others. Particularly if this question refers to all levels of government, people may have a difficult time answering the question. More important, the single question will oversimplify how people feel.

Two features of the summated rating scale will solve these problems. First, the use of more than two response choices will increase precision. Suppose people are asked

How do you feel about the government?

and are offered the following response choices:

Love it
Like it
Neither like nor dislike it
Dislike it
Hate it

Those who feel strongly can now be distinguished from those with more moderate feelings. The ambivalent respondents will be able to respond differently from respondents with definite tendencies toward one end of the scale or the other. Precision is greatly improved, and might be improved further with even more choices. Of course, in cases where respondents are able to answer only yes or no, more response choices will be ineffective. The key here is not to give respondents more choices than they are able to use.

Multiple items can address all three problems. People would respond to items concerning various aspects of government. They might be asked if they like the President, the Congress, the Supreme Court, and the Civil Service. They might be asked about services, taxes, how money is spent, and how the government is run. The variety of questions enlarges the scope of what is measured. It can be as broad or as narrow as the choice of questions.

Multiple items improve reliability by allowing random errors of measurement to average out. Given 20 items, if a respondent makes an error on one item, indicating "love it" instead of "hate it," the impact on the total score (the sum of all items) is quite minimal. In fact, errors in one direction will tend to cancel out errors in the other, resulting in a relatively constant total score over time. Reliability will be covered in greater detail later.

Finally, multiple items allow even more precision. With a single five-choice question, people can be placed into five groups on the basis of their responses. With 20 five-choice items, there are 61 possible scores ranging from 20 to 80, or over 16 times the precision (at least in theory).

What Makes a Good Scale?

A good summated rating scale is both *reliable* and *valid*. Reliability will be considered in two ways. First, *test-retest reliability* means that a scale yields consistent measurement over time. Assuming that the construct of interest does not change, each subject should get about the same score upon repeated testings. Second, *internal-consistency reliability* means that multiple items, designed to measure the same construct, will intercorrelate with one another. It is possible that a scale demonstrates only one of these types of reliability. Both types will be discussed at length in Chapters 5 and 7.

Reliability assures that a scale can consistently measure something, but it does not assure that it will measure what it is designed to measure. This property (that a scale measures its intended construct) is validity. There are many types of validity and several general approaches to establish it. These will be discussed in Chapter 6. Both reliability and validity are essential properties for a scale. Additional details on these topics are found in Carmines and Zeller (1979).

There are other things to look for in a good scale. First, items should be clear, well written, and contain a single idea. Many scales run into difficulty because items are ambiguous or contain multiple ideas. Unless absolutely necessary, jargon should be avoided. Colloquial expressions limit the use of the scale in terms of populations and time.

Another aspect of a good scale is that it is appropriate to the population of people who use it. Reading level, for example, must be considered with these scales. To make a scale broadly applicable, keep the items short and the language simple and straightforward. Concrete ideas produce the best items. Respondents should not have to guess what the intended meaning of an item might be. They should not miss the meaning of an item because they do not understand a word. Chapter 4 will cover the writing of good items.

Finally, a good scale is developed with concern for possible biasing factors. Personally sensitive items may evoke defensiveness on the part of some respondents. Scales measuring personal adjustment and psychopathology have long been known to suffer from distortion on the part of defensive respondents. Bias will be discussed in Chapter 4.

Steps of Scale Construction

The development of a summated rating scale is a multistep process. A thorough effort will involve conducting several separate studies. Figure 1.1 illustrates the five major steps in the process. First, before a scale can be developed, the construct of interest must be clearly and precisely defined. A scale cannot be developed until it is clear exactly what that scale is intended to measure. This may seem to be a simpleminded requirement, but it is at this step that many scale development efforts go astray. Too many scale developers spend insufficient time defining and refining the construct of interest.

Second, the scale itself is designed. This involves deciding on the exact format of the scale, including selection of response choices and writing of instructions. Item stems also are written at this step. The idea is to write an initial item pool, which will be subject to statistical analysis at later steps.

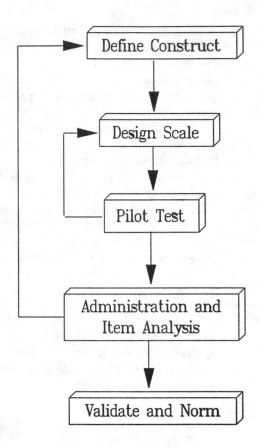

Figure 1.1. Major Steps to Developing a Summated Rating Scale.

Third, the initial version should be pilot-tested with a small number of respondents who are asked to critique the scale. They should indicate which items are ambiguous or confusing, and which items cannot be rated along the dimension chosen. The scale should be revised on the basis of the pilot respondents' feedback.

Fourth, the first full administration and item analysis is conducted. A sample of 100 to 200 respondents complete the scale. Their data are subject to an item analysis to choose a set of items that form an internally consistent scale. Coefficient alpha (Cronbach, 1951), a statistic representing internal-consistency reliability, is calculated. At this first stage, the essential property of reliability is established initially. If the items successfully produce an internally consistent scale, the final step can proceed. Otherwise, one must return to an earlier step to revise the scale.

Fifth, the scale is validated and normed. Traditionally, validity has been defined as the property that a scale measures its intended construct. (In other words, a valid scale measures what it was designed to measure.) As discussed later, this definition is an oversimplification, but for now this definition will be adopted.

At this step, a series of validation studies should be conducted to verify that the scale behaves as predicted. This step is much like theory-testing, in that relations of the scale with other variables are hypothesized. Data then are collected to verify the theoretical predictions. As evidence in support of validity is compiled, confidence is gained that the scale measures the theoretical construct it is intended to measure.

At the same time that validity data are collected, normative data also are collected. *Norms* describe the distributional characteristics of a given population on the scale. Individual scores on the scale then can be interpreted in relation to the distribution of scores in the population. Large samples of respondents can be used to estimate distributional characteristics (such as mean and standard deviation) of the population.

These five steps are essential for the development of a scale. Unfortunately, many scale developers do an inadequate job on the first and/or last steps. This is undoubtedly because these steps are the most difficult. Both rely on solid conceptual and theoretical thinking, based on the relevant research literature. Validation involves conducting research studies designed to test hypotheses about the scale. A good scale developer must first be a good researcher.

The remainder of this monograph will cover the steps involved in the development of a summated rating scale. This discussion will begin with the underlying classical test theory upon which such scales are based. Each of the steps in Figure 1.1 will be covered, including defining the construct, designing the scale, pilot-testing, conducting the item analysis, validating the scale, and establishing norms and reliability.

2. THEORY OF SUMMATED RATING SCALES

Before proceeding to the development of summated rating scales, it would be instructive to briefly review the theory behind them. The basic underlying idea derives from classical test theory, which provides the rationale for repeated, summated measurement.

Classical test theory distinguishes *true score* from *observed score*. A true score is the theoretical value that each subject has on the construct or variable of interest. An observed score is the score actually derived from the measurement process. It is assumed that each subject has a true score on the construct of interest. These true scores, however, cannot be directly observed. Rather, they are inferred from the observed scores. If one had perfectly reliable and valid measurement, the observed score would equal the true score.

According to classical test theory, each observed score is comprised of two components, the true score and random error. That is,

$$O = T + E,$$

where O is the observed score, T is the true score, and E is random error. Errors, by being random, are assumed to be from a population with a mean of zero. This implies that with multiple observations, errors will tend to average zero.

With a summated rating scale, each individual item is designed to be an observation of the intended trait. Each item represents an individual assessment of the true score. If the average (or sum) of individual items is calculated, the errors of measurement are assumed to average approximately zero, resulting in an estimate of the true score.

Errors of measurement are inversely related to reliability. For any given measurement situation, the larger the error component, the worse the reliability. Take the case of using a single item to measure a trait. Single items are notoriously unreliable, meaning that they have large error components. If errors are random, sometimes they will inflate and sometimes they will deflate the observed estimate of the true score. When repeated measurements are taken over time, there will be inconsistency (unreliability) in the observations. With multiple items combined into an estimate of the true score, errors will tend to average out, leaving a more accurate and consistent (reliable) measurement from time to time.

One way to increase reliability, therefore, is to increase the number of items. This is exactly the theory behind the summated rating scale—

use enough items to produce a reasonable level of reliability. The more error there is in individual items, the more items will be needed to yield good reliability for a total scale. With enough items, individual items need not be very reliable to yield a scale that is reliable overall. Of course, one should attempt to construct good items. It would be a mistake to produce large numbers of poor items under the assumption that errors will average out to zero. Although reliability may be achieved, poor items may not prove to be valid.

Achieving reliability merely means that the error components from the individual items have averaged out. Unfortunately, the use of multiple items does not guarantee that the true score measured was the true score intended. It is quite possible, and in many domains even likely, that the true score measured is not the trait that the scale was designed to assess.

Classical test theory is the underlying rationale behind the summated rating scale, as well as other types of measurement. However, classical test theory is an oversimplification and does not take into account other known influences on people's responses to such scales. The basic formula of classical test theory can be extended to include an additional component:

$$O = T + E + B,$$

where B is bias. Bias is comprised of systematic influences on observed scores that do not reflect the true score. Systematic influences are not random and do not come from distributions with means of zero. Thus they cannot be averaged out with multiple items. Bias represents an alternative trait or traits that influence observed score measurements.

One of the most troublesome sources of biases is *social desirability* (Crowne and Marlowe, 1964). Social desirability (or SD) is the tendency for some subjects to respond to items in a socially desirable or acceptable direction rather than giving their true feelings or responses to an item. For example, people high in SD will be unlikely to admit that they "cheat at card games" or "steal from family members." Thus for some people, the observed scores might reflect SD rather than, or in addition to, the trait of interest.

This is a particular problem in the measurement of personal adjustment and psychopathology. Many scales to measure such constructs contain items that are undesirable. Items concerning bizarre thoughts or behaviors (e. g., Do you hear voices? or Do you enjoy inflicting pain on others?) are likely to be problematic. If people score low on such scales, they might do so either because their true score on the trait is low or because they are high on social desirability and are hesitant to admit to undesirable things.

Research has been conducted on several sources of bias in responding to scales. Several have been described as *response sets,* which are tendencies for subjects to respond to items systematically. For example, *acquiescence response set* is the tendency for people to agree with all items regardless of the content. People who are high in acquiescence response set will score high on all items of a scale. Thus their scores will be uniformly inflated (assuming positively worded items). This is a constant inflation, and it cannot be handled merely by increasing the number of items.

Strategies have been developed for handling some of the known sources of bias. Biases cannot be completely eliminated, but they can be reduced. Social desirability, for example, can sometimes be reduced by carefully wording items to reduce their socially desirable content. Other types of scales, such as forced choice, have also been developed to handle social desirability.

Unfortunately, it is unlikely that all sources of bias are presently known. One can never be certain that these systematic influences have not influenced measurement. Scale developers proceed under the assumption that classical test theory represents a reasonably close approximation to their measurement situation. They recognize, however, that their scales may very well be contaminated by bias. Validation is essential in demonstrating that scales measure what was intended rather than bias.

3. DEFINING THE CONSTRUCT

One of the most vital steps in the development of a scale is the conceptual task of defining the construct. It almost goes without saying that a scale cannot be developed to measure a construct unless the nature of that construct is clearly delineated. When scales go wrong, more often than not it is because the developer overlooked the importance of carefully and specifically delineating the construct. Without a well-defined construct, it is difficult to write good items and to derive hypotheses for validation purposes.

One of the difficulties in social science research is that many constructs are theoretical abstractions, with no known objective reality. Such theoretical constructs may be unobservable cognitive states, either individual (e.g., attitudes) or shared (e.g., cultural values). These constructs may exist more in the minds of social scientists than in the minds of their subjects, whether their subjects are individual people or larger social entities.

If a construct is a theoretical abstraction, how then can one determine if a scale measures it? This is a difficult problem that undoubtedly has hindered progress in the social sciences. Validation is possible, but it must take place in a broad context of evaluating the usefulness of a construct, as well as its possible theoretical linkages to other constructs, some of which may be more objectively observable. A construct cannot stand alone, but only takes on meaning as part of a broader theoretical network that describes relations among many constructs. A construct cannot be developed in a vacuum. The problem of validation will be dealt with in greater depth in Chapter 6.

Many times not enough effort goes into conceptually developing a construct. This may be because the scale developers thought they had a good subjective impression of what the construct was. This approach is quite dangerous. When a construct is not defined carefully in advance, there is considerable risk that the scale will have poor reliability and doubtful validity. In other words, the connection between the construct and the scale will be unclear.

The approach strongly recommended here is an *inductive* one. The scale development effort begins with a clearly defined construct, and the construct definition guides the subsequent scale development. Much of the developmental work, particularly validation, takes a confirmatory approach, with theoretical ideas guiding the validation strategy. Hypotheses will be formulated about the relations of the scale to other variables. Validation research will be conducted to test those hypotheses.

An alternative approach some scale developers have taken is a *deductive* one. Items are administered to subjects, and complex statistics (e.g., factor analyses) are used in an attempt to uncover the constructs within the items. This is very much an exploratory approach, where the conceptual work is focused on interpreting results rather than formulating a priori hypotheses. Great caution must be used with this approach. Almost any group of correlated items is bound to result in factors that can be given meaning. The problem is that the constructs interpreted from analyses of the items may be more apparent than real.

A colleague once told me a story that illustrates how cautious one must be with exploratory approaches. When he was a graduate student, he witnessed several very senior and experienced researchers going over the results of a factor analysis. After some time they congratulated one another on a fine explanation of the results, which seemed at the time to be quite profound. About that time, the research assistant who conducted the analysis entered the room. With much embarrassment, he announced that the printout was in error. They were looking at no better than random numbers.[2] Interpretation of exploratory results must be done with great caution.

It is not that there is anything inherently wrong with factor analysis or exploratory research. For test construction, however, the inductive approach is preferred. Validation is a tricky and difficult business. It is that much more difficult when it is handicapped from the beginning by not being built on a solid conceptual foundation. Chapter 6 will discuss how factor analysis can be very useful as a validation strategy within the more inductive approach to scale development.

How to Define the Construct

Defining the construct may be the most difficult part of scale construction. This is particularly true with abstract and complex constructs. The conceptual work should begin with a general definition of the construct and then move to specifics. The more clearly delineated the construct, the easier it will be to write items to measure it.

In the delineation of a construct, it is helpful to base the conceptual and scale development effort on work that already exists. Unless the construct is totally new, there will be discussions and possibly empirical research in the literature. There also may be existing scales available to assess it. The existing literature should serve as a starting point for construct definition. Prior conceptual definitions and operationalizations of the construct can provide a solid foundation. Often a scale development effort can help refine a popular construct that has not been sufficiently developed in the literature.

The first step to construct definition is a literature review. One should carefully read the literature about the construct, paying attention to specific details of exactly what the construct has been described to be. If the construct is popular, chances are there are several different definitions of it. To develop a scale, a definition must be adopted. These various definitions of a construct undoubtedly will be discussed in the context of broader theories. The construct cannot be described in a vacuum; it must exist within a network of relations between it and other constructs. If the conceptual/theoretical work is well done, not only will the items be easy to write, but the framework for validation will be specified as well.

Take the construct of stress, for example. There are many stress theories, leading to different conceptions about what stress is, and many stress scales. Some researchers consider stress to represent particular environmental conditions. A death in the family or a job with a heavy workload both represent stress. Others consider people's emotional reactions to be stress. Feeling depressed (perhaps because of a death in the family or being overworked) would be stress. Still others consider physiological reactions to be stress. Increased heart rate, higher blood pressure, and a suppressed immune system all would be stress according to this view. The exact procedures or scales used to measure stress are going to be dependent upon the definition of exactly what stress is. The environment might be measured through observation, emotion by the person's self-report, and physiology with appropriate medical tests. The same general methodology could not be used to measure all three conceptions because they represent different kinds of constructs, even though they all are called stress.

Attempts to define stress precisely have run into difficulties. Initially, attempts were made to adopt a purely environmental definition of stress and to specify what sorts of environmental conditions are stress and what sorts are not. A death in the family can be considered an environmental stress. To deal with individual differences in reactions to events like family death, some researchers broadened their definition to include the survivor's feelings about the deceased. If the survivor hated the family member and was happy that he or she died, the death would not be considered an instance of stress. The survivor must be upset by the death for it to be considered stress. If the survivor's feelings are important, then the person's emotional reactions are in part defining stress, and the definition includes both environment and emotion. Now the definition is not purely environmental but deals with the individual's response to the environment.

As can be seen, the process of construct definition can be complex and become quite convoluted. Stress was chosen purposely as an example, because it is a construct that has defied satisfactory conceptual development. This has led many stress researchers to abandon stress as a construct. Instead, stress is used as the name of a topic area. Research strategies have focused on determining relations among more specific constructs. Family-member death, feelings about the deceased, and reactions to the death all can define separate constructs that can be investigated in relation to other variables of interest. For example, research has focused on how family-member death affects the health of survivors.

If scales exist to measure the construct of interest, the content of these existing scales may help scale development. It is not unusual to develop a scale out of existing scales. This may be done in domains where a high quality scale does not exist. The items from several scales can be used as a starting point in writing an initial item pool. These would be modified and more items added to create the item pool from which the final scale will be developed.

The most difficult situation is where no conceptual or empirical work has been done on a construct. With nothing upon which to build, the construct and scale probably will evolve together. It may take several attempts at scale development until the construct is well enough developed to be useful.

Homogeneity and Dimensionality of Constructs

Constructs can vary from being highly specific and narrowly defined to being multidimensional. Some constructs are quite simple and their content can be covered adequately with a single item. Others are so complex that they may be broken down into several subconstructs. The content of complex constructs can only be adequately covered by a scale with multiple subscales.

A person's feelings about a consumer product are a rather homogeneous construct. One might ask people to sample a new cracker and ask them whether or not they like it. For a market researcher, if liking relates to future purchasing, this level of specificity may be quite sufficient. For other uses, however, perhaps it is not. Liking might be subdivided into components, such as liking the flavor, liking the texture, liking the shape, liking the color, and liking the odor. Even this simple construct can be subdivided.

Other constructs are far more complex. Job satisfaction has been shown to be comprised of several components, most of which do not intercorrelate highly. Employees can be satisfied with some aspects of jobs and not others. One individual may like the pay but dislike the boss. Another person may like the nature of the work but dislike co-workers. Most scales to measure job satisfaction contain subscales to assess some of these components, although different scale developers have chosen different components.

Part of construct definition is deciding how finely the construct is to be divided. With multiple-item scales, one could consider each item to be a separate dimension or aspect of the construct. The whole idea of the summated rating scale, however, is that multiple items are combined rather than analyzed separately. Even where multiple-item subscales are developed, different scale developers will disagree about how many different aspects of the construct should be defined.

The ultimate answer about how finely to divide a construct must be based on both theoretical and empirical utility. If subdividing a construct adds significantly to the explanatory power of a theory, and if it can be supported empirically, then subdividing is indicated. If the theory becomes overly complex and unwieldy, or empirical support cannot be found, then subdividing should not be done. In science, the principle of *parsimony* should be followed—that is, the simplest explanation among equal quality explanations is the one that is adopted.

Theoretical Development of Work Locus of Control

Locus of control is a personality variable that has been very popular in psychology and other social sciences. Rotter (1966) defined locus of control as a generalized expectancy about reinforcements in life. Some people believe that reinforcements (rewards and punishments) are under their own personal control; others do not share this belief. Although locus of control is assessed along a continuum, theoretically *internals*, who believe that they have personal control, are distinguished from *externals*, who believe that luck, fate, or powerful others control their reinforcements.

Following Phares's (1976) recommendation, I decided to develop a scale to measure a domain-specific locus of control scale for the work setting. The first step in its development was to review the literature on general locus of control, paying particular attention to studies conducted in the work setting. The characteristics and behaviors of internals and externals described in the literature were carefully considered. Some of these characteristics were derived purely from theory; others came from studies that contrasted the two personality types. Also considered were the particular reinforcers that would be relevant in the work domain.

According to the working definition, extended from the more general construct, *work locus of control* concerns generalized expectancies about control of reinforcements or rewards at work. Internals feel they can control reinforcements at work; externals feel they cannot. Externals attribute control to luck, fate, or powerful others, most typically superiors. The items were written from this description of the construct and specification of the characteristics of internals and externals. Compared to the stress example, this project was not very difficult. An advantage here was that the general construct, from which work locus of control was developed, was itself well developed. There was a rich theory and extensive literature from which to draw. However, this does not guarantee that the scale will prove scientifically or practically useful, or that it will measure what it is intended to measure. The value of the conceptualization will become apparent only through validation and continued research use of the WLCS.

4. DESIGNING THE SCALE

Construct definition, if properly done, leads easily into the next step of scale design. There are three parts to be completed. First, there are the number and nature of the response choices or anchors. Second, there are the item stems themselves. Finally, there are any special instructions that are to be given to the respondents.

Response Choices

The first thing to be decided in constructing the response choices is the nature of the responses respondents are to make. The three most

TABLE 4.1

Response Choices for Agreement, Frequency, and Evaluation Scales

Agreement Response Choice	Frequency Scale Value	Evaluation Response Choice	Scale Value	Response Choice	Scale Value
Slightly	2.5	Rarely	1.7	Terrible	1.6
Moderately	5.4				
Inclined to	5.4	Seldom	3.4	Inferior	3.6
Very much	9.1	Sometimes	5.3		
		Occasionally	5.3	Passable	5.5
		Most of the time	8.3	Good	7.5
				Excellent	9.6

common are *agreement, evaluation,* and *frequency.* Agreement asks subjects to indicate the extent to which they agree with items. Evaluation asks for an evaluative rating for each item. Frequency asks for a judgment of how often each item has, should, or will occur.

Agreement response choices are usually bipolar and symmetrical around a neutral point. Respondents are asked to indicate if they agree or disagree with each item, as well as the magnitude of their agreement or disagreement. Response choices might ask subjects to indicate if they "strongly," "moderately," or "slightly" agree and disagree. The modifiers would be the same for both agree and disagree, making the response choices symmetrical. Although it is not necessary, many scale developers will include a neutral point, such as "neither agree nor disagree."

Spector (1976) calculated psychological scale values for popular modifiers for agreement, evaluation, and frequency. This was accomplished by having raters (college students) rank lists of modifiers. The rank data were converted to psychological scale values using mathematical procedures described in Guilford (1954). Table 4.1 shows approximately equally spaced agreement modifiers for all three types of response choices. Although equally spaced modifiers may not be essential (Spector, 1980), respondents may have an easier time with a scale if they are.

Agreement response anchors are quite versatile and are the most popular. Items can be written to assess many different types of variables, including attitudes, personality, opinions, or reports about the environment. Table 4.1 offers three choices, which will produce a six-point scale.

Evaluation choices ask respondents to rate along a good-bad dimension. Choices in Table 4.1 range from positive (*excellent*) to very negative (*terrible*). There is no middle response. Evaluation response choices can be used to measure attitudes or to evaluate performance. Faculty evaluation forms, for example, often ask students to evaluate their instructors on several dimensions.

Frequency scales ask respondents how often or how many times something has happened or should happen. Some researchers have argued for the superiority of giving numeric anchors, such as *once per day* or *twice per day* (e.g., Newstead and Collis, 1987), but most scales seem to use verbal anchors. Table 4.1 contains a set of anchors ranging from *rarely* to *most of the time*. Some scales use *never* and *always* to anchor the ends of a scale. Frequency response choices commonly are used to measure personality in scales where respondents indicate how often they have engaged in certain behaviors. They also are used to measure characteristics of environments, where respondents indicate how often certain events occur.

For many constructs, any of these response choices will work. For others, one might be preferable over others. Suppose one is interested in people's voting behavior. To determine how often people engage in certain voting-related behaviors, it probably makes the most sense to use frequency items. For example, one item might ask subjects

How often do you vote in primary elections?

Response choices might be "always," "sometimes," or "never."

This question can also be handled with agreement items, but not as efficiently. Consider the following series:

I always vote in primary elections.

I sometimes vote in primary elections.

I never vote in primary elections.

Respondents would indicate extent of agreement with each. As long as they are consistent, strongly agreeing only with one item, the same information can be obtained. However, agreement requires more items and may produce ambiguous results if respondents agree (or disagree) with what seem like mutually exclusive items.

Evaluation also could be used, but again not as well. Consider the following question:

How good is your voting record in primary elections?

A problem here is interpreting what a respondent might think constitutes a good or bad voting record. One person may consider voting half the time to be good, and another consider it to be bad.

Frequency has somewhat the same problem in that response choices may not mean quite the same thing to all people (Newstead and Collis, 1987). However, frequency gets more directly at how often people do the behavior in question, whereas evaluation gets more at how they feel about it. The exact nature of the construct of interest would determine which makes most sense to use.

Another decision to be made is the number of response choices. One might suppose that more choices would be better, because more choices allow for greater precision. This is certainly true, and some scale developers have used over 100. One must consider the measurement sensitivity of the person who is completing the scale. As the number of response choices increases, a point of diminishing returns can be quickly reached. Although there are some minor differences in opinions, generally between five and nine choices are optimal for most uses (e.g., Ebel, 1969; Nunnally, 1978).

Table 4.1 can be used to help select response choices that are approximately equally spaced. For each choice, the table also provides its scale value. The table does not contain all possible anchors, or necessarily the best anchors. They are offered as a starting point for anchor selection. Additional anchors can be found in Spector (1976).

Quantifying Response Choices

Response choices are chosen so that they can be ordered along a measurement continuum. Frequency varies from nonoccurrence (none or never) to constant occurrence (always or continually). Evaluation varies from as poor as possible to as good as possible. Agreement is bipolar, ranging from total disagreement to total agreement. Regardless of the response choices, they must be ordered from low to high, and numbers must be assigned to each choice.

For some constructs, it is possible to vary from zero to a high positive value. Such scales are *unipolar*. For other constructs, it is possible to have both positive and negative values, with a zero point somewhere in the middle. These scales are *bipolar*. Frequency of occurrence is unipolar because there cannot be fewer than zero occurrences of a phenomenon. Attitudes are often bipolar, because one can have positive, neutral, or negative attitudes.

With unipolar scales, response choices are numbered consecutively from low to high, beginning with 1 from low to high. Thus, a five-point scale would range from 1 to 5. Bipolar scales can be numbered the same way. Some scales use both positive and negative numbers for bipolar scales. A six-point scale would range from -3 to $+3$, with disagree responses getting negative numbers and agree responses getting positive numbers. If there is a neutral response, it would be assigned a 0.

A total score for a scale would be calculated by adding the numbers associated with responses to each item. If both positively and negatively worded items are used, the negatively worded items must be reverse scored. Otherwise, the two types of items will cancel each other out. For a scale ranging from 1 to 5, negatively worded items would have scaling reversed. Hence, $5 = 1$, $4 = 2$, $3 = 3$, $2 = 4$, and $1 = 5$.

There is a formula that accomplishes the reversal:

$$R = (H + L) - I,$$

where H is the largest number, L is the lowest number, I is response to an item, and R is the reversed item. For the five-choice example, if a respondent scores a 2 for an item,

$$R = (5 + 1) - 2$$

or

$$R = 4.$$

Writing the Item Stems

The second step in scale design is writing the item stems. The phrasing of the stem is dependent to a large extent upon the type of judgment or response people are asked to make. Agreement items are declarative statements that one can agree with or not. Examples could include the following statements:

The death penalty should be abolished.

I like to listen to classical music.

I am uncomfortable around strangers.

Frequency items are often events, circumstances, or behaviors that make sense to indicate how often they occur. Respondents might be asked how often the following occur:

Candidates for president make campaign promises they know they cannot keep.

You exercise strenuously enough to raise your heart rate.

Your husband helps with the housework.

Evaluation items are often words or short phrases representing persons, places, things, events, or behaviors that a person can evaluate. Items to evaluate might include the following:

Police services in your neighborhood.

The softness of the facial tissue you just tried out.

How well your favorite sports team played last week.

A good item is one that is clear, concise, unambiguous, and as concrete as possible. It also should make sense in relation to the nature of the response choices. Writing good items is an essential part of scale development. Below are five rules to consider in writing good items. Although there may be circumstances in which one or more of these rules will be violated, they should be carefully considered when writing items.

1. *Each item should express one and only one idea.* When more than one idea is expressed in an item, respondents can become confused.

They may find their response to each different idea in the item is different. Consider the following item:

My instructor is dynamic and well organized.

This item asks about two separate instructor traits—dynamism and organization. How does a person respond if his or her instructor exhibits only one of the traits? In fact, these traits may be reciprocally related. Many dynamic people are rather loose and disorganized. Often well-organized people are not very outgoing. A respondent attempting to rate an instructor who is high on only one trait would be unsure how to respond and may (a) agree with the item because the instructor exhibits a high level of one characteristic; (b) give a middle response to the item, averaging the responses to both ideas; or (c) strongly disagree with the item, because the item asked about an instructor who is high on both traits and the instructor in question was high on only one. Quite likely, respondents will differ in how they respond to this item, making the item invalid. For every item, carefully consider if it contains one and only one idea. Two ideas should be placed into two items.

2. *Use both positively and negatively worded items.* One of the ways in which bias can be reduced is by using items that are phrased in opposite directions. If a scale asks people how they feel about something, some items should be favorable and some unfavorable. For example, if a scale is designed to assess attitudes about welfare, some items should be written in a favorable direction (e.g., "Welfare provides a valuable service to needy people") and others should be written in a negative direction (e.g., "Welfare is responsible for many of our social problems"). A person who has a favorable attitude should agree with the first item and disagree with the second. A person with an unfavorable attitude should have the opposite pattern of responses.

By varying the direction of questioning, bias produced by response tendencies will be minimized. One such tendency is acquiescence—the tendency for respondents to agree (or disagree) with items regardless of content. A person exhibiting such a tendency will tend to agree (or disagree) with both of the above items regardless of how he or she feels about them. If all items are written in one direction, acquiescent respondents will have extreme scores on the scale—either very high or very low. Their extreme scores will tend to distort estimates of the mean and the results of statistical tests conducted on the scale scores. If there are an equal number of positively and negatively worded items, acquiescent respondents will tend to get middle scores. Their scores will do far less damage to estimates of means and results of statistical tests.

With both types of items, acquiescence will become apparent. One can calculate separate scores for items in each direction. Each respondent will have a positively worded item score and a negatively worded item score. Respondents who score high on both or low on both are probably exhibiting acquiescence. It should be noted, however, that acquiescence has not always been shown to be a problem with summated rating scales (e.g., Rorer, 1965; Spector, 1987).

3. *Avoid colloquialisms, expressions, and jargon.* It is best to use plain English (or whatever language is being used), avoiding terms that will limit the scale to a particular population. Unless the scale has a particular circumscribed use, it is best to keep the language as generalizable as possible. Even widely known expressions may limit the use of the scale to certain groups and to a limited time span. An American expression, for example, may not be understood by subjects in other English-speaking countries, such as England or Australia. The problem becomes worse if the scale is to be translated into another language.

One also should consider that words tend to change both meaning and connotation over time. Expressions may be particularly prone to time-constrained meanings. Consider the possibility of developing a scale about abortion opinions. An item such as "I support the pro-life position" will be understood by most people to mean anti-abortion. There may be a new pro-life movement that has nothing to do with abortion 10 or 20 years from now, and few people will associate pro-life with anti-abortion. Unless the scale is specifically concerned with opinions about the pro-life movement itself, which would have to be described by the specific name, it would be best to use a more general item. An example might be "I feel abortion should be illegal."

4. *Consider the reading level of the respondents.* Another point, related to the prior one, is that respondents should be able to read and understand the items. Be sure that the reading level and vocabulary are appropriate for the respondents. A scale developed for college students may not be appropriate for high school, simply because the vocabulary level is too high. Also consider the complexity of the items. Highly educated groups may be quite comfortable with complex, abstract ideas in items. Less educated groups may not fully understand the same items. Unfortunately, most respondents will not complain. Instead, they

will do the best they can, producing error and bias when they fail to understand the items. Consider that the simpler and more basic the language, the broader will be the appropriate population of people who can provide good data.

For those who do not read, a scale can be administered orally. This should be done cautiously, however. An oral version should be developed separately. One should not assume that the oral version will have the same psychometric properties as the written. At a minimum, the item analysis should be conducted on a sample of respondents who were administered the scale orally.

5. *Avoid the use of negatives to reverse the wording of an item.* It is very common to reverse the wording of an item by adding a negative, such as "not" or "no." The positively worded item "I am satisfied with my job" can be made negative by adding "not":

I am not satisfied with my job.

The difficulty with the negatives is that they are very easy for a respondent to miss. In working with scales with these types of items, I have noticed that many people seem to misread the negated items. In other words, they respond to a negative on the same side of the response scale as the positive.

A missed negative reverses the meaning of an item and leads to a response that is at the wrong end of a scale. Of course, this type of error is the reason for using multiple items. The total score will be only slightly changed by a single error. However, these errors do reduce the reliability of a scale.

It is usually quite easy to produce an item without the negative. In this case, for example, the reworded item would be

I hate my job.

When people read this item, it is not very likely that they will mistake its meaning for its opposite.

Instructions

A final thing that might be included in a scale is instructions. Instructions can cover two main issues. First, respondents can be given direc-

TABLE 4.2

Instructions for the Work Locus of Control Scale (WLCS)

The following questions concern peoples' opinions and beliefs about jobs and careers. These questions refer to *jobs in general* and not the job you presently have or a particular job you once had. These questions ask about your personal beliefs, so there are no right or wrong answers. No matter how you answer each question, you can be assured that many people will answer it the same way.

For each of these questions please indicate your agreement or disagreement. You should do this by circling the number that most closely represents your opinion about that question. If you find that you disagree very much, circle a 1; if you disagree moderately, circle a 2; if you disagree slightly, circle a 3. Conversely, if you agree very much, circle a 6; if you agree moderately, circle a 5; and if you agree slightly, circle a 4.

Remember, answer these job-related questions for *jobs in general* and not one particular job.

---

tions for using the scale. This may not be necessary for many respondent groups, such as college students, who are used to completing such scales. It will be necessary for people who are unfamiliar with summated rating scales, because it will not be very obvious to them what they should do with the scale. An example of the instructions for the WLCS is in Table 4.2.

The second type of instruction is specific to the particular construct. It may be necessary to instruct subjects about the judgment task they are being given. For example, instructions can tell them to whom or what the items refer. With a generic scale measuring attitudes about a politician, instructions would indicate which politician to consider.

Instructions also can give respondents a common frame of reference. In this case, a person or thing that would be obviously very high or very low on the scale would be described. For example, with a job-autonomy scale, it might be suggested that a college professor is very high and a factory worker very low. Details would be given about how professors have very unstructured jobs allowing them almost total personal control. Conversely, factory workers would be described as being very constrained in most aspects of work. These two extremes give all respondents a more or less common basis from which to judge their own jobs. Of course, individuals will interpret the descriptions from their own idiosyncratic frames of reference. Instructions should reduce at least some of the idiosyncrasy and will hopefully reduce error.

Response choices also can be defined more specifically. For example, with a frequency scale ranging from *seldom* to *quite often,* it could be noted that in this circumstance a frequency of once a day would be considered "quite often" and once a month would be "seldom."

Designing the WLCS

The work locus of control construct is concerned with people's beliefs about control at work. It seemed most appropriate for the scale to contain statements with which respondents could indicate agreement. A six-point scale was chosen, with three response choices on the agree end and three on the disagree end. Table 1.1 contains the scale, including the response choices and final 16 items.

The original item pool had 49 items: 21 written in the internal direction, and 28 in the external direction. The procedures used to reduce the scale to its final 16-item version are discussed in the next chapter.

Instructions (shown in Table 4.2) were included to indicate that the items refer to jobs in general and not a particular job. This is important because work locus of control is conceptualized to be a characteristic of the respondent rather than his or her job. Although there is no guarantee that the respondents will use this frame of reference in answering the questions, the phrase "jobs in general" was italicized and mentioned twice. Also, the wording of many items was designed to refer to jobs in general. Some items, however, might be interpreted for a particular job.

Instructions were included for using the scale as well. This was not necessary for the initial college student sample, but because the scale was being developed for a broader, employed sample, the instructions were included. Undoubtedly they would be necessary for some respondents who might be asked to complete the scale in the future.

Half the items shown in Table 1.1 are in the external direction and half are in the internal. To score the scale, half the items must be reversed. After reversal, a total score would be calculated as the sum of the 16 items. Because the six response choices were numbered from 1 to 6, total scores can range from 16 (1×16) to 96 (6×16). In keeping with Rotter's (1966) general locus of control scale, high scores represent the external end of the scale and low scores represent the internal end.

5. CONDUCTING THE ITEM ANALYSIS

This next step in scale construction requires the collection of data so that an item analysis can be conducted. Its goal is to produce a tentative version of the scale—one that is ready for validation. With careful attention to the prior steps, and a little luck, this step will only have to be conducted once. Otherwise the initial item pool will fail to converge on an internally consistent scale, making it necessary to return to a prior step. This might involve reconceptualization of the trait or the writing of additional items.

To conduct this step in scale development, the scale must be administered to a sample of respondents. It is helpful if the respondents are as representative as possible of the ultimate population for which the scale is intended. This is not always possible, and many scales are developed initially on college students because they are readily available. In such cases care must be taken in using the scale on a noncollege-educated sample. It is possible that the new sample's responses will differ, perhaps because the reading level is too high.

The item analysis requires a sample size of about 100 to 200 respondents. The initial sample for the WLCS was 149. This size sample is usually easily attained in a university setting. In other settings or with specialized populations it may be more difficult to obtain this number of respondents. Far more respondents will be needed for later stages of scale development.

The data analysis involves statistics no more complex than correlation coefficients, but they would be very time consuming if done by hand. SPSS-X includes an item-analysis routine that can conduct the item analysis discussed in this chapter. It is widely available in both the mainframe and microcomputer versions. Directions for using the program will be provided later in this chapter.

Item Analysis

The purpose of an item analysis is to find those items that form an internally consistent scale and to eliminate those items that do not.

Internal consistency is a measurable property of items that implies that they measure the same construct. It reflects the extent to which items intercorrelate with one another. Failure to intercorrelate is an indication that the items do not represent a common underlying construct. Internal consistency among a set of items suggests that they share common variance or that they are indicators of the same underlying construct. The nature of that construct or constructs is certainly open to question.

The item analysis will provide information about how well each individual item relates to the other items in the analysis. This is reflected by the *item-remainder* coefficient calculated for each item. (This statistic also is called the *part-whole* or *item-whole* coefficient.) The item-remainder coefficient is the correlation of each item with the sum of the remaining items. For a scale with 10 items, the item-remainder for Item 1 would be calculated by correlating responses to Item 1 with the sum of responses to Items 2 through 10. The item-remainder for Item 2 would be calculated by correlating responses to Item 2 with the sum of Item 1 and Items 3 through 10. This would continue for all 10 items.

If the items are not all scaled in the same direction—that is, some are positively and some are negatively worded—the negatively worded items must be reverse scored. Otherwise responses to the positive items will cancel out responses to the negative items, and most subjects will have a middle score. For each item, a high score should represent a high level of the construct, and a low score should represent a low level. Thus respondents who are high on the construct will agree with the positively worded items and disagree with the negatively worded. To score them properly, the extent of agreement should equal the extent of disagreement. For a six-point scale, a 6 for agreement of a positively worded item should equal a 1 for disagreement of a negatively worded item. Strongly agreeing with the item

I love milk

is more or less equivalent to strongly disagreeing with the item

I hate milk.

With six-point scales, a subject would be given a score of 6 for strongly agreeing with the first item, and a score of 6 for strongly disagreeing with the second. (See Chapter 4 for more on item reversal.)

The item analysis will provide an item-remainder coefficient, which is a correlation, for each item. Those items with the highest coefficients are the ones that will be retained. There are several strategies for deciding which items to retain. If it is decided that the scale should have m items, then the m items with the largest coefficients would be chosen. Alternately, a criterion for the coefficient (e.g., .40) can be set, and all items with coefficients at least that great would be retained. Both strategies can be used together—that is, retaining up to m items, providing they have a minimum-sized coefficient.

There is a trade-off between the number of items and the magnitude of the item-remainder coefficients. The more items, the lower the coefficients can be and still yield a good, internally consistent scale. Internal consistency involves the next statistic, coefficient alpha.

Coefficient alpha (Cronbach, 1951) is a measure of the internal consistency of a scale. It is a direct function of both the number of items and their magnitude of intercorrelation. Coefficient alpha can be raised by increasing the number of items or by raising their intercorrelation. Even items with very low intercorrelations can produce a relatively high coefficient alpha, if there are enough of them.

The reason for this goes back to classical test theory. If all items are assumed to reflect a single underlying construct, then the intercorrelations among items represent the reciprocal of error. In other words, the part of each item that does not correlate with the others is assumed to be comprised of error. If there is relatively little error, the items intercorrelate highly. It will not take many items to make the error average out to approximately zero. If, on the other hand, the intercorrelations are small, error is quite large. It will average out, but many items will be needed for it to do so.

Keep in mind, however, that classical test theory provides several assumptions that may or may not hold in actuality. Low intercorrelations among many items may produce an internally consistent scale, but this does not guarantee that the items reflect a single, underlying construct. If we were to take two scales that measure correlated but distinct constructs, a combination of all their items might well yield internal consistency, even though they reflect two different constructs. The statistics generated by an item analysis are good guides to item selection, but item content must be examined closely in drawing conclusions about what is being measured.

Coefficient alpha reflects internal-consistency reliability, which does not necessarily reflect reliability over time. Scales that measure constructs (such as mood) that fluctuate over time may be internally consistent but yield low reliability over time.

The values of coefficient alpha look like correlation coefficients, but alpha is not a correlation. It is usually positive, taking on values from 0 to just under 1.0, where larger values indicate higher levels of internal consistency. Nunnally (1978) provides a widely accepted rule of thumb that alpha should be at least .70 for a scale to demonstrate internal consistency. Many scales fail to achieve this level, making their use questionable at best. It is possible to find a negative coefficient alpha if items correlate negatively with one another. This occurs if items are not properly reverse scored. Assuming all items have been scored in the proper direction, alpha should be positive.

Coefficient alpha involves comparison of the variance of a total scale score (sum of all items) with the variances of the individual items. Mathematically, when items are uncorrelated, the variance of the total scale will be equal to the sum of variances for each item that comprised the total scale.

As the items become more and more intercorrelated, the variance of the total scale will increase. For example, suppose a scale has three uncorrelated items. The total scale will be the sum of the three items. If the three items each have a variance of 1.0, the total scale will have a variance of 3.0. If the items correlate with one another, the total scale will have a variance that is larger than 3.0, even though the individual items still have variances of 1.0.

The formula for coefficient alpha is

$$\alpha = \frac{k}{k-1} \times \frac{s_T^2 - \Sigma s_I^2}{s_T^2}$$

where s_T^2 is the total variance of the sum of the items, s_I^2 is the variance of an individual item, and k is the number of items. As can be seen, the numerator of the equation contains the difference between the total scale variance and sum of the item variances. The ratio of this difference to the total score variance is calculated. The result is multiplied by a function of the number of items.

In choosing items for a scale, one uses both item-remainder coefficients and coefficient alpha. A series of steps may be involved, deleting

TABLE 5.1
Illustration of Using the Item Analysis to Select Items

Step	Item	Item-Remainder Coefficient	Alpha if Item Removed
1	1	.53	.68
	2	.42	.70
	3	.36	.71
	4	.10	.74
	5	.07	.75
	6	−.41	.80
	7	.37	.71
	8	.11	.79
	9	.55	.68
	10	.42	.70
		Coefficient Alpha = .72	
2	1	.56	.79
	2	.43	.81
	3	.31	.84
	7	.39	.82
	9	.58	.78
	10	.44	.81
		Coefficient Alpha = .83	
3	1	.57	.79
	2	.44	.80
	7	.40	.80
	9	.59	.79
	10	.45	.80
		Coefficient Alpha = .84	

some items, checking alpha, deleting more items, and rechecking alpha, until a final set of items is chosen. Deleting "bad" items tends to raise alpha, but reducing the number of items tends to lower it. Deleting many weak items may or may not raise the coefficient alpha, depending upon how many items are left and how weak the deleted items were.

Table 5.1 presents a fictitious example of the process, where 10 items were administered to a sample of respondents. Step 1 in the table shows the item remainders for each item, ranging from −.41 (for Item 6) to .55 (for Item 9). Beneath these coefficients is the overall coefficient alpha for the scale (in this case, .72). In addition, the last column of the table shows the coefficient alpha, with each item removed. This is helpful in that it shows, for each individual item, what effects its removal will have on the scale's internal consistency.

Six of the items have item-remainder coefficients greater than .35, and each will cause a decrease in coefficient alpha if removed. The remaining four items will result in an improved coefficient alpha if removed. Interestingly, Item 6 has a rather large coefficient, but it is negative. Possibly a scoring error was made, and this item should have been reverse scored. If this is the case, the error should be fixed and the analysis rerun. It often occurs, however, that an item that seemed to be worded in one direction yields a large negative coefficient. In this case the item is not behaving as intended. Something is obviously wrong, requiring careful examination of the item.

Whenever there are large negative item remainders, all the prior steps should be examined carefully. One should check that no errors have been made and that the scale development effort has not gone wrong at this point.

The first thing to consider with a negative item remainder coefficient is that the item might be poorly written. Often an item that initially seemed reasonable may in fact be ambiguous. A second possible problem is that the item was inappropriate for the current respondents. They may have been incapable of understanding the item or may not have had information necessary to properly respond to it. If the items and respondents are not the problem, perhaps there were weaknesses in the conceptualization of the construct. Returning to the conceptualization step to consider if the construct has been properly defined would seem warranted. Perhaps the construct itself has no validity, or the conception of it is incorrect. For example, it may have been hypothesized that a certain personality characteristic would be reflected in correspondence among several behaviors. The data may have indicated, however, that these behaviors did not occur together (at least as reflected by respondent reports). These data would raise questions about the viability of the construct in question.

Some scale developers rely on empiricism to determine the direction of item wording. This is a dangerous procedure likely to result in scales with doubtful validity. The item analysis should not be used to determine the direction in which items should be scored. The exception is when the item analysis finds an error in scoring direction, as discussed above. Items tend to behave erratically when their scoring direction is reversed. Positive item-remainder coefficients can become negative when another item's sign is changed. It can take many iterations of sign reversals before they will all stay positive. Even though an acceptable coefficient alpha may be achieved, the validity of the scale will be called into question, because the conceptual foundation is weak and the items may be of poor quality. It is also likely that the items assess multiple constructs. There are no shortcuts to devising good scales.

Assuming that Item 6 in the Table 5.1 example was a badly written item, it is eliminated, along with Items 4, 5, and 8. Step 2 shows an improvement in the scale. Coefficient alpha increased to .83, and the scale is more efficient, only needing 6 items instead of 10. Notice that five items had item remainders that increased slightly. One (Item 3) declined from .36 (Step 1) to .31 (Step 2). Its removal will increase alpha somewhat to .84. It is removed in Step 3, and the scale has been reduced to five items, with an alpha of .84. Note that each of the five items will reduce alpha if removed.

There is one puzzling outcome of these results, and that involves Item 3. Surprisingly, its item-remainder coefficient declined when the "bad" items were removed in Step 2. This can happen because of the complex pattern of intercorrelations among items. Although this item correlated with the final five items in the scale, it also correlated with at least some of the deleted items. In this case, it correlated more strongly with the deleted items than the retained. Hence, when the items were deleted, the contribution of Item 3 declined. Removing it improved the scale.

The discussion here of coefficient alpha was necessarily brief. For additional detail the interested reader might consult a psychometrics text (e.g., Allen and Yen, 1979; Nunnally, 1978).

External Criteria for Item Selection

Internal consistency is the most frequently used criterion for item selection. An alternative approach, sometimes used in conjunction with internal consistency, is to select (or delete) items based on their relations with external (to the scale) criteria. In other words, items are retained when they relate to a variable of interest, or items are deleted when they relate to a variable of interest.

When there is a concern about bias, one strategy is to independently measure the bias and then remove items that relate to it. Operationally, this would involve administering the scale to a sample while measuring the biasing variable on the same people. Each item would be correlated with the biasing variable. Assuming that the items vary in their relations with the biasing variable, only those with small (or no) relations would be chosen.

A common external criterion for item selection is social desirability (SD; Crowne and Marlowe, 1964). From a scale-development perspective, SD reflects an individual's tendency to respond to scale items in a socially desirable direction. Individuals who exhibit a high level of SD will tend to agree with favorable items about themselves (e.g., "I never hesitate to go out of my way to help someone in trouble") and will tend to disagree with unfavorable items about themselves (e.g., "I can remember 'playing sick' to get out of something"). Both of these items are from the Crowne-Marlowe SD scale (Crowne and Marlowe, 1964).

Each item for the scale under development can be correlated with scores on SD. Items that significantly correlate with it would be deleted from the final scale. In this way a scale can be developed that is free of SD bias. That is, responses to the scale will be unaffected by SD of respondents. Of course, with some constructs, it will not be possible to write items that are independent of SD. This might occur because the construct itself is related to the underlying construct of SD. In this case, the validity of the scale will be open to question. Is it measuring the intended construct or SD?

If things go as planned, once the item-selection process is complete, an acceptable, internally consistent scale will be achieved. A tentative version of the scale is now ready for the next stage of development. Additional work needs to be done to replicate the item analysis on a second sample, to further establish reliability, and to validate. These tasks can be accomplished concurrently.

When the Scale Needs More Work

There is no guarantee that the scale will achieve sufficient internal consistency in the initial attempt. There may be several items that meet the criteria for item retention, but coefficient alpha may be too small. If this is the case, additional items need to be written, more data need to be collected, and the item analysis needs to be redone. This situation can occur when there were too few items initially or when many of the items were of poor quality. It also can happen because the conceptual framework for the construct was weak.

The first question when an acceptable level of internal consistency is not achieved is whether the problem was with the construct definition or with the items. This question is difficult to answer definitively. Some clues may be provided by an inspection of the items that were retained and the items that were deleted. It may become apparent that the intended construct was too broad or too vaguely defined. For example, suppose a unidimensional construct was thought to contain four related elements, and items were written to reflect each of them. If the items reflecting each element of the construct failed to interrelate, the item analysis might retain too few items to achieve an internally consistent scale. Perhaps the construct is narrower than thought, and it should focus on only one of the four elements. Conversely, the construct might be multidimensional, with each element representing a separate facet. Such a situation would necessitate the development of subscales.

A careful examination of deleted items might suggest that they were just poor items. They may have contained some of the problems discussed in Chapter 4. Alternatively, they may have been inappropriate for the respondent group. One way to explore these possibilities would be to interview several respondents about their reactions to and interpretations of the individual items.

When the item analysis results in too few items, it is helpful to estimate the number of items that must be added to achieve an acceptable level of internal consistency. The *Spearman-Brown prophesy formula* can be helpful in estimating the number of additional items that should be needed to achieve a given level of internal consistency. Given the coefficient alpha for a specified number of items, the prophesy formula indicates the effects on alpha of increasing or decreasing the number of items. It is based on the assumption that the added or deleted items are of the same quality as the initial or retained items. If they are not, the formula may over- or underestimate the number of items.

The formula can estimate the level of coefficient alpha that will be achieved if the number of items is increased or decreased by a specific factor. For example, what will alpha be if the number of items is doubled or halved? The formula can be turned around to indicate by how much the scale length must be increased or decreased to achieve a given value of coefficient alpha.

TABLE 5.2
Reliabilities as a Function of Adding and Deleting Items According
to the Spearman-Brown Prophesy Formula

Initial Alpha	Changing Length by a Factor of					
	.25	.33	.50	2	3	4
.50	.20	.25	.33	.67	.75	.80
.60	.25	.33	.43	.75	.82	.86
.70	.37	.44	.54	.82	.88	.90
.80	.50	.57	.67	.89	.92	.94
.90	.69	.75	.82	.95	.96	.97

The prophesy formula is

$$r_N = \frac{k \times r_O}{1 + (k-1) \times r_O}$$

where r_N is the reliability (coefficient alpha) of the new length, r_O is the reliability of the old length and k is the factor by which the scale is being increased or decreased (e.g., 2 to double the length or 0.5 to divide it in half).

Table 5.2 shows the effects of increasing and decreasing a scale by a factor of 1/2, 1/3, 1/4, 2, 3, and 4. Several representative values of coefficient alpha are illustrated, from .50 to .90. From the table it can be seen that for a scale with a coefficient alpha of .70, doubling the number of items raises coefficient alpha to .82 and halving the number of items decreases coefficient alpha to .54.

The prophesy formula can give a target number of items for the final scale. Say the initial item pool began with 15 items and after the item analysis wound up with only 5 items, with a coefficient alpha of .60. The formula (see Table 5.2) indicates that the number of items must be doubled to achieve a coefficient alpha of .75 and tripled to achieve a coefficient alpha of .82. Assuming that the new items would be equivalent in quality to the original and that only one third of the items would be retained, another 15 to 30 items would be needed. Of course, a careful inspection and analysis of the nature of the retained and discarded items should help improve the quality of items written for the second effort. A larger proportion of items should be retained the second time.

The prophesy formula also can be used to reduce the number of items. Say there is a 30-item scale with a coefficient alpha of .90. The scale may be too long, and considering its high internal consistency, it certainly could be shorter. Table 5.2 shows that reducing the scale by one half (to 15 items) results in a coefficient alpha of .82. Again this assumes that the retained and deleted items were equally reliable items. If item-analysis data were available, the 15 best items would be retained, making the .82 a lower bound to the coefficient alpha that might be achieved.

Multidimensional Scales

So far this discussion has focused on development of unidimensional scales, based on fairly homogeneous, unidimensional constructs. Many constructs, however, are quite broad and may contain multiple aspects or dimensions. Attitudes toward complex things (such as government, jobs, families, and life in general) can contain many facets. To adequately express their attitudes and opinions, people may need multiple dimensions, reflected in multiple subscales.

The development of multidimensional scales is not much different from their unidimensional counterparts. On the conceptual end, the various components are specified. These components do not have to be unrelated, and often subscales of multidimensional instruments intercorrelate. Conceptually they should be distinct, however.

The procedures discussed so far in developing unidimensional scales would be followed, with each subscale developed in parallel with the others. Items would be written to assess each intended facet. The items are usually mixed up in the initial item pool. They would all be administered to the same respondent sample. An item analysis would be conducted separately for each subscale, including only items for that subscale. Often all items are analyzed for a total score, but this is only done when it makes conceptual sense to do so.

It is best with multidimensional scales if each item is part of one and only one subscale. There are several reasons for this. First, in designing subscales, it is assumed that the construct is complex enough to be represented by conceptually separate components. If the content of the components overlap to the extent that subscales must share items, they are probably not separate enough to warrant separate components.

From a measurement perspective, shared items cause some difficulties. Perhaps most important, comparisons among components reflected in subscales become ambiguous. Inferences about underlying construct relations will not be possible. In other words, do subscales correlate because their underlying constructs are related or because they share items? Likewise, when different subscales correlate with another criterion variable, it will not be possible to attribute similar relations to the underlying constructs or to item overlap.

This also can be a problem when items on subscales, although not identical, contain similar content. Content overlap can occur because two constructs share common components. Take the emotional states of anger and anxiety. People can distinguish between these emotions, but they share some common characteristics. They both involve increased arousal that is aversive. Items like "I feel tense," "I feel bad," or "I feel uncomfortable" are likely to reflect both emotions.

If overlapping items are eliminated, the content validity of the scale may be compromised in that it may not reflect the entire scope of the construct. If the overlapping items are retained, the interpretation of relations among scales may be compromised. This is because each scale has items that reflect another construct. If a respondent is high in anxiety but not anger, that person will score high on the overlapping items that are on the anger scale. The anger score will be inflated because of anxiety. The correlation between both scales will be inflated to some degree because of subjects who are high on only one construct. If a correlation between the anxiety and anger scales is observed, care must be taken not to misinterpret the reason. Do subjects who experience one emotion tend to experience the other, or does each scale reflect the other emotion to some extent? Answers to this type of question are not easy to find.

With this example, it might be expected that anxiety and anger are distinct enough that overlapping items could be avoided. Perhaps respondents could be asked just to rate how anxious and angry they are, assuming that nonanxious angry people will not report experiencing anxiety, and nonangry anxious people will not report experiencing anger. Other constructs may not be as easily distinguished. Nicholls et al. (1982) discussed how overlap at the construct level can be unavoidable and problematic to interpretation of data.

During construct development, care should be taken to determine where constructs overlap and where they are distinct. Part of the development of a new construct is to show how it differs from existing constructs. During scale construction, an effort should be made to avoid overlap in content between the new scale and other scales, unless that overlap is intended because underlying constructs overlap. Where scales share item content, care should be taken in interpretation of their intercorrelations.

Conducting Item Analysis with SPSS-X

Although not absolutely necessary, the use of computers to conduct item analysis is strongly recommended. Even with relatively few items, an item analysis will take many hours to conduct by hand. With the widespread availability of computers and appropriate software, it would be foolish to avoid the computer.

One of the most popular statistical software packages that can be used for item analysis is SPSS-X (SPSS Inc., 1988). Both mainframe and microcomputer versions exist, and at least one or both are available at most, and probably all, universities in the United States. The "reliability" routine can be used to conduct item analysis. It provides the item statistics and coefficient alpha that were discussed earlier. It is also capable of more sophisticated analyses, which are beyond the scope of this monograph.

Table 5.3 contains the program statements to conduct the item analysis for the WLCS. Omitted are the system commands for running this analysis on a mainframe computer, because these commands differ from computer to computer. It also should be noted that computer software tends to change over time. It is possible that the commands shown here will not work on a future version of the program.

This example assumes that the original 49 items of the WLCS were entered on a single data line for each individual respondent. Each data line, representing a single respondent, has a respondent identification number (ID) in columns 1 to 3. The 49 items are listed in order from columns 4 to 52, and are named X1 to X49.

The first line of the program specifies where the data are located. This example is from the IBM PC-compatible microcomputer version. The data were in a file on the A drive called "A:WLCS.DAT." The second line of the program indicates the names of the variables and where on each data line they were located. The next eight lines are compute statements to reverse the scoring of the appropriate items. Only the first

TABLE 5.3
Control Statements to Run SPSS-X Item Analysis

DATA LIST FILE 'A:WLCS.DAT' FIXED
  /ID 1-3 S1 TO S49 4-52.
  COMPUTE S1 = 7 - S1.
  COMPUTE S2 = 7 - S2.
  COMPUTE S3 = 7 - S3.
  COMPUTE S4 = 7 - S4.
  COMPUTE S7 = 7 - S7.
  COMPUTE S12 = 7 - S12.
  COMPUTE S15 = 7 - S15.
  COMPUTE S16 = 7 - S16.

       .
       .
       .

RELIABILITY
  /VARIABLES S1 TO S49
  /SCALE(WLCS) S1 TO S49
  /MODEL ALPHA
  /SUMMARY TOTAL.

---

eight are shown here. The next line invokes the reliability routine. Below it is the variables statement that lists all items, whether or not they are all to be item analyzed. In this case, it lists items X1 to X49. The next line determines the type of analysis, names the scale (WLCS), and indicates the items to be chosen. In this example all items have been selected, although smaller subsets are allowable. With multidimensional scales this command specifies the items for the particular subscale. The next line specifies the model, which in this case is alpha. This tells the program to conduct the type of item analysis discussed here. These last two lines would be repeated to conduct item analyses on subscales. Each pair specifies a different subset of items, corresponding to a subscale. The final line indicates the statistics to be calculated. There are many possible options, all of which are well described in the SPSS-X manual (SPSS Inc., 1988).

As can be seen, the analysis itself is quite easy to conduct with the computer. When items are deleted from step to step, the variables and scale commands in the program are changed, listing only those items to be retained.

Table 5.4 is a sample of the output from the reliability routine, run with the microcomputer version. To save space, only the first and last six items are shown. The output includes the features discussed above. The program is capable of producing many additional things. The program first lists the items that are included in the analysis. Below that is a table summarizing the item statistics. Included for each item is the mean for the total scale with the item deleted, the variance for the total scale with the item deleted, the item-remainder (item-total) coefficient, and coefficient alpha with the item deleted. Below this table is the coefficient alpha. (Note that this is the microcomputer version. The mainframe version provides additional information, none of which has been discussed here.)

Item Analysis on the WLCS

The initial item pool for the WLCS contained 49 items. It was administered to 149 undergraduate students, who served as the initial development sample. Because locus of control is a personality variable, there was concern about the possible biasing effect of social desirability. The Crowne-Marlowe SD scale (Crowne and Marlowe, 1964) was included in the questionnaire so it could be used as an external criterion for item selection. In addition, the questionnaire contained several scales and items that could be used for validation, assuming the items formed an internally consistent scale. These will be discussed in Chapter 6.

Items were written in both an internal and an external direction. The original plan was to balance the scale with an equal number of each item type. The rationale for this approach was that biases introduced by wording direction would balance out as much as possible.

The coefficient alpha for all 49 items was .86, which is acceptable. However, a 49-item scale was considerably longer than desired. Considering that 28 items had item-remainder coefficients greater than .295, the scale could be reduced in length considerably. Chosen for the final scale were the best eight external items and the best eight internal items. All of the external items had higher item-remainders than the internal items. This might suggest that the internal items could be eliminated. They were not because the initial plan was to balance the two item types. Coefficient alpha was acceptable with both types of items.

TABLE 5.4

SPSS-X Item-Analysis Output for the Work Locus of Control Scale (WLCS)

Reliability Analysis—Scale (WLCS49)

1.	S1
2.	S2
3.	S3
4.	S4
5.	S5
6.	S6
.	.
.	.
.	.
44.	S44
45.	S45
46.	S46
47.	S47
48.	S48
49.	S49

RELIABILITY ANALYSIS—SCALE (WLCS49)

Item-Total Statistics

	Scale Mean If Item Deleted	Scale Variance If Item Deleted	Corrected Item— Total Correlation	Alpha If Item Deleted
S1	137.4631	418.5071	.2975	.8753
S2	138.6913	418.7959	.2703	.8758
S3	138.8926	419.6506	.3013	.8752
S4	138.9262	415.0688	.3835	.8739
S5	138.9866	419.2971	.2493	.8762
S6	139.5436	415.3173	.3701	.8741
.	.	.	.	.
.	.	.	.	.
S44	138.4228	420.8403	.2756	.8755
S45	138.1275	412.8553	.4524	.8729
S46	139.3020	417.1041	.5143	.8730
S47	139.9732	425.7155	.2357	.8760
S48	138.3356	420.0623	.2124	.8771
S49	139.0671	417.8333	.4390	.8736

Reliability Coefficients
N of Cases = 149.0 N of Items = 49
Alpha = .8769

TABLE 5.5
Item Analysis of the Work Locus of Control Scale (WLCS)

Item Number	Direction of Wording	Initial Item Remainder	Final Item Remainder
1	Internal	.35	.29
2	Internal	.34	.30
3	Internal	.41	.35
4	Internal	.30	.24
5	External	.52	.52
6	External	.56	.59
7	Internal	.31	.32
8	External	.55	.50
9	External	.62	.64
10	External	.62	.68
11	External	.52	.54
12	Internal	.34	.34
13	External	.59	.64
14	External	.50	.56
15	Internal	.48	.46
16	Internal	.44	.43

A correlation was calculated between each of the 49 items and the SD scale. It was decided to eliminate any item that correlated significantly with SD; however, no items had to be eliminated for this reason.

Table 5.5 contains the item-remainder coefficients for the final 16 items of the scale. Shown here for each item is the wording direction, the item-remainder coefficients from the 49-item analysis, and the item-remainder coefficients from the final 16-item analysis. The item-remainder coefficients ranged from .30 to .62 in the initial analysis of all 49 items. The item-remainder coefficients changed somewhat when the analysis was recomputed on the 16 items. The item-remainder coefficients tended to decline for the internally worded items and tended to increase for the externally worded items. The final item-remainder coefficients ranged from .24 to .68.

Although the removal of two items actually would have slightly improved the scale's coefficient alpha, they were not removed in order to keep the internal and external items balanced. An alternative strategy would have been to eliminate these two items (which were both written in the internal direction) and also eliminate two external items. When this was done, the coefficient alpha for the scale was even lower.

Hence, the 16 items were retained. The coefficient alpha for the entire scale was .845. This was somewhat lower than the total 49-item scale, but still within the range of acceptable reliabilities.

At this point a tentative version of the WLCS that demonstrated acceptable internal consistency was achieved. Social desirability, a major potential source of bias, appeared to be minimized. The scale seemed ready for the next step of validation, but the comparatively lower item-remainder coefficients for the internally worded items were troubling. We will return to this issue in Chapter 6.

6. VALIDATION

The most difficult part of scale development is validation—that is, interpreting what the scale scores represent. If it is internally consistent, the scale certainly measures something, but determining the nature of that something is a complex problem. Part of the difficulty is that validation can only occur within a system of hypothesized relations between the construct of interest and other constructs. Tests for validity involve simultaneous tests of the hypotheses about constructs and hypotheses about scales.

As discussed earlier, many constructs in the social sciences are theoretical abstractions that do not exist in objective experience. How, then, can there be a valid measure of a construct when the construct itself cannot directly be validated? A complete answer to this question is beyond the scope of this discussion and involves issues that fall in the domain of the philosophy of science.

The typical scale-validation strategy involves testing the scale of interest in the context of a set of hypothesized interrelations of the intended construct with other constructs. That is, hypotheses are developed about the causes, effects, and correlates of the construct. The scale is used to test these hypotheses. Empirical support for the hypotheses implies validity of the scale.

Validation of a scale is like the testing of a theory, in that its appropriateness cannot be proven. Instead, evidence is collected to either support or refute validity. When a sufficient amount of data supporting validity is amassed, the scale is (tentatively) declared to be construct valid. Users of the scale will accept the theoretical interpretation of what it represents. Of course, the underlying construct is very much a theoretical entity. The conception of the nature of the construct and the reasons why it relates to other constructs are grounded in a theoretical framework that may in the future be replaced by a new framework redefining the construct.

As with a theory, a construct is tentatively accepted because it is useful. That is, a useful construct is part of a theoretical system of relations with other constructs that may explain, predict, and lead to control over phenomena of interest. Empirical validation evidence provides support for theoretical predictions about how the construct of interest will relate to other constructs. It demonstrates the potential utility of the construct.

The validation effort cannot occur until after the item analysis has been conducted and the items are chosen. Data relevant to validation can be collected at the time the initial item pool is administered. Assuming that early validity studies look promising, the scale would continue to be used in studies designed, at least in part, to provide validity data.

Techniques for Studying Validity

In this chapter three different approaches to establishing validity will be discussed. *Criterion-related validity* involves the testing of hypotheses about how the scale will relate to other variables. *Discriminant* and *convergent* validities are frequently studied together and involve investigating the comparative strengths or patterns of relations among several variables. Both of these approaches to validity involve the studying of hypothesized relations between a scale of interest and other variables. Factor analysis will be covered as a means of exploring the dimensionality of a scale.

Criterion-Related Validity. There are several types of criterion-related validity, all involving comparing scores on the scale of interest with scores on other variables, or *criteria*. Such comparisons involve correlating scores on the scale of interest with scores on other variables. They also involve comparing different identifiable groups of respondents on the scale of interest.

A criterion-related validity study begins with the generation of hypotheses about relations between the construct of interest and other constructs. Often a scale is developed for the purpose of testing an existing, well-developed theory. In this case the scale can be validated against the hypotheses generated by the theory. Other times a scale is developed to assess a construct that may not be part of a well-developed theory. In this case, theoretical work must be done to generate hypotheses about the construct. In either case, criterion-related validity must be based on hypotheses. The best situation is when data already exist to support the hypotheses. Conclusions about validity can be more confidently made when confirming data about the underlying constructs already exists.

Concurrent validity can be tested by simultaneously collecting data from a sample of respondents on the scale of interest and on criteria, hypothesized to relate to the scale of interest. Concurrent in this context refers to the simultaneous collection of all data. Hypotheses are typically that the scale of interest will correlate with one or more criteria. The finding that there are statistically significant relations of the scale with hypothesized variables is taken as support for validity.

Predictive validity is much the same as concurrent, except that data for the scale of interest are collected before the criterion variables. Thus it is a test of how well the scale can predict future variables. An advantage of a predictive-validity study over a concurrent is that it better demonstrates how well a scale can predict a future variable under time intervals that mirror the situation in which the scale might actually be used in the future. An example is the prediction of respondents' quitting from an activity, such as a job or school, as predicted by their personality or attitudes.

To conduct a concurrent-validation study, it is common to embed the scale of interest in a questionnaire that contains measures of several variables. Multiple hypotheses are tested with this strategy. Of course, with several hypotheses it is likely that one or more will *not* be supported. This is particularly likely when the hypotheses are not grounded in a well-supported theory. It is in this situation that the interdependence of theory and scale validation is most apparent. Scale developers often will claim validity if at least some hypotheses have support, particularly those that may be crucial. They conclude (or perhaps merely hope) that some of their hypotheses were wrong, rather than that their scale lacked validity.

This case requires a judgment call, weighing the criticality of each hypothesis to the establishment of validity. Some hypotheses may be so central to the construct that failure to support them damages the case for validity of either the scale or the construct. Of course, one cannot rule out the possibility that the empirical test itself was flawed. Perhaps the data used to test the scale, often derived from other scales, were invalid. Perhaps biases or confounds in the design of the study affected the results. Perhaps the test lacked sufficient statistical power due to small sample size.

Known-groups validity is based on hypotheses that certain groups of respondents will score higher on a scale than others. The main difference between this type of validity and the other two is that the criterion in this case is categorical rather than continuous. Means on the scale of interest can be compared among respondents who are at each level of the categorical variable. Although the statistics used are not correlation coefficients, mean differences still reflect relations between the scale and the categorical criterion variable.

To conduct a known-groups validity study, hypotheses must specify which groups will score higher on the scale than other groups. For example, a hypothesis might state that Republicans will score higher, on average, than Democrats on a scale of political conservatism. Likewise, it might be hypothesized that corporate executives will score higher on a scale of job complexity than data-entry clerks.

The next step is to identify groups of respondents and administer the scale to them. The groups would be statistically compared to determine if the means differ as expected. *T* tests or analyses of variance would be used (depending upon the number of groups compared) to determine if the differences were statistically significant.

The availability of groups determines the nature of the known-groups comparisons that can be made. Often groups that should score high or low may not be readily accessible. For example, people with a rare health disorder, people who have been in jail, or people who are former U.S. senators may be very difficult to find. Known-groups studies are designed with these limitations in mind.

There are two critical features of all criterion-related validity studies. First, the underlying theory from which hypotheses are drawn must be solid. It is quite a difficult task to conduct both theory- and scale-validation tests concurrently. When things go wrong, as they frequently do, it cannot be determined if the problem was in the theory or in the scale. Second, in order to conduct a good validity test of a scale, there must be good measurement of the criterion. Failure to find expected relations with criteria may well reflect criterion invalidity rather than scale invalidity. Confidence must be high in the validity of the criterion before conclusions can be drawn about scale validity.

Convergent and Discriminant Validity. Convergent validity means that different measures of the same construct will relate strongly with one another. Discriminant validity means that measures of different constructs should relate only modestly with one another. These two types of validity are studied in relation to one another, where the relative magnitude of relations within constructs versus across constructs is hypothesized. That is, a scale will correlate more strongly with another measure of the same construct than it will correlate with measures of different constructs. The underlying idea is that a construct should relate more strongly to itself than to another construct.

Convergent validity can be indicated by comparing scores on a scale with an alternative measure of the same construct. It is expected that the two measures will correlate strongly. Ideally they should correlate at about the level of their reliabilities. In other words, two valid measures of a construct should relate almost perfectly, if they are both perfectly reliable. Because there is always some degree of error depressing reliability, observed correlations among alternate measures of the same construct will be depressed to some extent.

The ability to assess convergent validity is dependent upon the existence of alternative measures. With some constructs such alternatives may exist, but with others they may not. In some domains there may be well-established scales that can serve as standards against which new scales can be evaluated. Despite the prior existence of an adequate scale, a new scale may be developed for a particular respondent group or for a specific purpose. Its validity would be tested against the more general standard.

Campbell and Fiske (1959) provided the Multitrait-Multimethod Matrix (MTMM) for simultaneously exploring convergent and discriminant validities. The use of this tool requires that at least two constructs are measured, and each has been measured with at least two separate methods. This last requirement can greatly limit where the tool can be used, because it is not always possible to measure constructs with multiple methods.

The MTMM is best explained with an example. (Additional details and examples can be found in Campbell and Fiske, 1959.) The validity study from which this example comes involves comparing a new meas-

TABLE 6.1

Multitrait-Multimethod Matrix for Three JSS Versus JDI Subscales

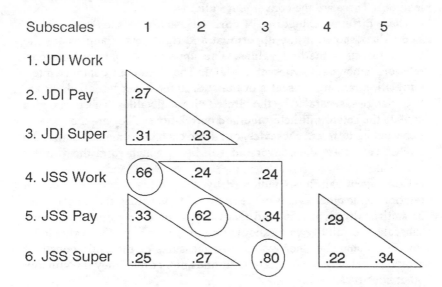

Subscales	1	2	3	4	5
1. JDI Work					
2. JDI Pay	.27				
3. JDI Super	.31	.23			
4. JSS Work	.66	.24	.24		
5. JSS Pay	.33	.62	.34	.29	
6. JSS Super	.25	.27	.80	.22	.34

ure of employee job satisfaction with an existing standard. The Job Satisfaction Survey (JSS; Spector, 1985) is a nine-subscale instrument designed to assess people's satisfaction with and attitudes about various facets of their jobs. It was developed specifically for use with employees of human service organizations, such as hospitals, mental health centers, or social service agencies. In the job satisfaction domain, there exists a well-validated and widely used scale called the Job Descriptive Index (JDI; Smith et al., 1969). Five of the subscales of the JSS are also included in the JDI. Both scales were administered to a sample of 102 employees (see Spector, 1985, for more details). The availability of data from the same respondents for both scales allowed an MTMM analysis, considering each scale as a separate method.

Table 6.1 is an MTMM matrix of three subscales: satisfaction with the nature of work tasks, pay, and supervision. The matrix contains the intercorrelations of all six variables (the three JDI scales and the three JSS scales). Analysis of the matrix involves separating the correlations into three categories. First, there are the correlations across subscales within each instrument. These are the heterotrait-monomethod correlations. Next, there are the correlations across subscales across instruments.

These are the heterotrait-heteromethod correlations. Finally, there are the correlations between subscales measuring the same trait but across methods. These are the convergent validities.

These different categories of correlations can be seen in the table. The values shown in the uppermost and rightmost triangles are the heterotrait-monomethod values. The uppermost contains intercorrelations among subscales of the JDI. The rightmost contains intercorrelations among subscales of the JSS. In the lower left quadrant are two triangles, separated by the circled diagonal values. These triangles contain the heterotrait-heteromethod correlations. They are the correlations among different subscales, one from each instrument. Finally, the circled values are the convergent validities, which form the validity diagonal.

Convergent validity is indicated by the validity diagonal values in relation to the other values in the matrix. These values should certainly be statistically significant and relatively large in magnitude. For each subscale, the validity value should be larger than any other value in its row or column. In other words, two measures of the same construct should correlate more strongly with one another than they do with any other construct.

Discriminant validity is indicated by lower correlations in the triangle areas than the circled convergent-validity values. Each triangle contains corresponding comparisons for each pair of subscales compared. For example, every triangle indicates the correlation between pay and supervision scales. The rank orders of these correlations (within each triangle) should be the same across triangles.

The values in the table indicate good convergent and discriminant validities for the JSS. The validity diagonal values are all rather large (from .62 to .80) and are the largest values in the entire matrix. Corresponding correlations within each triangle are quite similar and are rather modest, ranging from .22 to .34. These rather small values suggest that the subscales are assessing different constructs.

The Campbell and Fiske (1959) subjective method of evaluating the matrix works quite well in circumstances like this one, where validity for all scales is quite clear-cut. In other cases, deviations from the ideal case may make their method difficult to use. Quite a few statistical methods are available to evaluate MTMM matrices (see Schmitt and Stults, 1986). Perhaps the most popular recently is the use of structural equation modeling (Long, 1983; Widaman, 1985). This technique can be quite useful, but it has some serious limitations (Brannick and Spector, 1990; Marsh, 1989). The recent development of direct product models shows promise, although few applications can be found (e.g., Bagozzi and Yi, 1990; Wothke and Browne, 1990). For scale-development purposes, inspection of the matrix itself can give strong hints about potential validity problems that may exist in some subscales and not in others.

Use of Factor Analysis
for Scale Validation

Factor analysis can be quite useful for validating both unidimensional and multidimensional scales. For unidimensional scales, factor analysis can be used to explore possible subdimensions within the group of items selected. With multidimensional scales, factor analysis can be used to verify that the items empirically form the intended subscales.

Two basic types of factor analysis can be used for scale development. *Exploratory factor analysis* is useful for determining the number of separate components that might exist for a group of items. *Confirmatory factor analysis* allows the testing of a hypothesized structure. Such is the case when the items of subscales are tested to see if they can support the intended subscale structure.

A detailed discussion of factor analysis itself is well beyond the scope of this monograph. Many sources exist on both types, including Kim and Mueller (1978a, 1978b) for exploratory factor analysis and Long (1983) for confirmatory factor analysis. However, there are some basic aspects of these techniques to keep in mind in the discussion of their use for scale development.

The basic idea of factor analysis is to reduce a number of items to a smaller number of underlying groups of items called *factors*. For example, a scale containing 50 items might reduce to 5 factors, each containing 10 items. These factors can be indicators of separate constructs or of different aspects of a single rather heterogeneous construct. It can be difficult to decide which situation has occurred when looking at the results of a factor analysis alone.

Factor analysis derives its factors by analyzing the pattern of covariation (or correlation) among items. Groups of items that tend to interrelate with one another more strongly than they relate to other groups of items will tend to form factors. The idea here is somewhat like convergent and discriminant validity. Items that intercorrelate relatively high are assumed to reflect the same construct (convergent validity), and items that intercorrelate relatively low are assumed to reflect different constructs (discriminant validity). If all items correlate strongly with one another at about the same magnitude, a single factor will be produced. This suggests that a single construct is being measured by the scale.

One feature of factor analysis to bear in mind is that the results are a function of the items entered. The relative strength or proportion of variance accounted for by factors is a function of the nature and number of items that were selected. With a multidimensional scale, those subscales with more items will tend to produce stronger factors that account for more variance. Subscales with very few items will tend to produce very weak factors. Poor items and response biases can wreak havoc with a factor solution.

Exploratory Factor Analysis. Exploratory factor analysis is a good technique for studying the dimensionality of a scale, either a (supposedly) unidimensional or a multidimensional one. Because the goal of this analysis is usually to explore the dimensionality of the scale itself, principal components would seem a reasonable factor analytic model to use, although other models are also available.

Two major questions must be addressed with a factor analysis: (a) the number of factors that best represent the items and (b) the interpretation of the factors. Although factor analysis is a mathematical procedure, the answer to these two questions falls in the realm of subjective judgment as much as in the realm of statistical decision rules.

The analysis itself involves several iterative steps. First, the principal components are derived, with one component or factor derived for each item analyzed. Each of these initial factors will be associated with an *eigenvalue*, which represents the relative proportion of variance accounted for by each factor. There will be one eigenvalue for each item, and the sum of the eigenvalues will equal the number of items. If the items do not correlate with one another, the eigenvalues will reflect only the variance in the original items and each will be equal to 1.0. This indicates that the items do not cluster into factors. As the items intercorrelate more and more strongly, they will produce factors that contain more and more of the variance in the items, and the initial eigenvalues will become larger than 1.0. If all items are perfectly correlated, they will produce a single factor that will have an eigenvalue equal to the number of items. The other eigenvalues will equal zero. If the items form several factors, each will have an eigenvalue greater than one, indicating that it is accounting for more variance than a single item.

Once it is determined how many factors exist, an orthogonal rotation procedure is applied to the factors. Rotation procedures are designed to produce clusters of items based on various mathematical criteria (see Kim and Mueller, 1978a). Several choices exist, but they all result in a loading matrix (or matrices) that indicates how strongly each item relates to each factor. A loading matrix contains statistics (factor loadings) that are correlations of each original variable with each factor. Every variable (represented as rows in the matrix) has a loading for every factor (represented as columns of the matrix). It is hoped that each variable will have a large loading on one and only one factor. A variable is said to "load" on that factor for which it has a high loading. A minimum value of about .30 to .35 is required to consider that an item loads on any factor.

One difficulty with the factor-analysis procedure is that subjective judgment is necessary to determine the number of factors and their interpretation. Several procedures exist to determine the number of factors (see Kim and Mueller, 1978a). These procedures involve the eigenvalues that reflect the amount of variance accounted for by each factor.

A strategy many researchers use is to rotate several different numbers of factors and rely on meaningfulness of interpretation to decide on the number of factors. One might factor analyze 30 items, and based on the eigenvalues decide to rotate three, four, and five factors. In each case, the items in each factor would be subjectively scrutinized to determine if they form a conceptually meaningful factor. It might be found that only the three-factor solution results in factors that make conceptual sense.

At this point the interpretation of results has become very much a subjective, conceptual process. A scale intended to be unidimensional may well appear to have multiple subscales. In a statistical sense, the results indicate that items form multiple clusters, based on the relative strengths of relations among them. This can occur because the scale is measuring multiple constructs, or because the construct is heterogeneous, containing several components. Whether it is better to use the scale unidimensionally or multidimensionally is not always a simple question.

For example, take the construct of anxiety. Anxiety contains both cognitive (e.g., feeling afraid) and physical (e.g., palms sweating) components. Some anxiety scales contain items relating to both. Should the two components be separated, or are they both indicators of the same underlying construct? The answer lies in the researcher's purpose. If the purpose is to investigate the impact of anxiety on a person's task performance, separating the components is probably of little utility. If, on the other hand, the researcher is studying the anxiety response itself, there may be an interest in separating the components.

From a scale-development point of view, the conclusion that factors represent different constructs must be based on validation. The factor analysis can suggest that factors may exist, but additional validation evidence must be collected. In the final analysis, if the individual factors all have the same correlates, they cannot be discriminated on the basis of criterion-related validity. It is hard to argue that they represent separate constructs when they cannot be differentiated on the basis of their relations with other constructs. Under these circumstances, the law of parsimony suggests that the simpler, unidimensional conclusion should be drawn.

For multidimensional scales, one should empirically test if factors form the original subscales. To accomplish this, one should select the number of subscales as the number of factors to rotate. The solution will indicate how well the data fit the intended structure of the scale. This needs to be done with some caution, however. Factor analysis results can be quite sensitive to the total set of items that are included. Adding and deleting a single item can have profound effects on the results. Failure to find that the factor structure exactly fits subscales is quite common. One must consider the extent to which the factor structure deviates, and if it suggests that the subscales are seriously in error.

Another caution concerns the finding of trivial factor-analysis solutions. Finding a factor structure with very few items for each factor (e.g., one or two) generally is not very useful. Factor analysis is not likely to be useful on scales with few items.

The Job Satisfaction Survey (JSS; Spector, 1985) provides an example of how factor analysis can be used with multiple subscale instruments. This scale was designed to measure nine aspects of job satisfaction. Four items for each subscale were chosen on the basis of an item analysis. An exploratory factor analysis was conducted to ascertain if the nine subscales would be supported. It was found that only

TABLE 6.2
Pay and Supervision Factor Loadings for the
Job Satisfaction Survey (JSS)

Item	Subscale	Factor 1	Factor 2
I feel I am being paid a fair amount for the work I do.	PAY	.07	.77
My supervisor is quite competent in doing his or her job.	SUP	.80	.05
When I do a good job, I receive the recognition I should receive.	REW	.46	.25
Raises are too few and far between.	PAY	.03	−.54
My supervisor is unfair to me.	SUP	−.73	−.06
I do not feel that the work I do is appreciated.	REW	−.33	−.27
I feel unappreciated by the organization when I think about what they pay me.	PAY	−.08	−.73
My supervisor shows too little interest in the feelings of subordinates.	SUP	−.76	−.08
There are few rewards for those who work here.	REW	−.11	−.39
I feel satisfied with my chances for salary increases.	PAY	.08	.56
I like my supervisor.	SUP	.77	−.01
I don't feel my efforts are rewarded the way they should be.	REW	−.17	−.48

NOTE: SUP = Supervision; REW = Rewards.

eight eigenvalues were greater than 1.0. Furthermore, when nine factors were rotated, it was apparent that some of the subscales broke down. That is, each factor did not contain the four items from one subscale.

Inspection of the eigenvalues suggested that at most only eight factors were represented in the data, and eight were rotated. Six of the eight subscales were supported by the factor structure. Factors 3 to 8 contained only four items, and for each of these six factors, the four items came from only one subscale. Results for Factors 1 and 2 were more complex. The loading matrix for these two factors and the items that loaded on them are shown in Table 6.2. The items themselves are listed in the first column of the table. The name of the subscale from which each item came is listed in the second column. Items loading on the first two factors came from only three of the nine subscales. These were satisfaction with pay (PAY), satisfaction with supervision (SUP), and general availability of rewards (REW). Loadings on the first and second factors are listed in the third and fourth columns, respectively. Negative loadings occurred for the negatively worded items because their scoring was not reversed.

As can be seen, the four supervision items loaded only on Factor 1, and the four pay items loaded only on Factor 2. The rewards items split. The last two loaded only on Factor 2. The first one loaded only on Factor 1. The second reward item loaded more strongly on Factor 1 than Factor 2, but the difference was not very great (-.33 versus -.27). Note that this item violated one of the five rules for good items by using a "not" to change wording direction.

These results suggest that the JSS contains eight rather than nine dimensions. The items from one subscale collapsed into two of the others. In view of these results, one might be tempted to delete the Contingent Rewards subscale and place its items into the Pay and Supervision scales. Interestingly, adding these items to the two other subscales did not appreciably raise their coefficient alphas, even though there were six rather than four items. Another possibility would be to delete the subscale, under the assumption that it merely measured a combination of two other subscales (in other words, it is redundant and unnecessary). At the current time the subscale remains in the instrument. If future research fails to demonstrate its usefulness, it will be deleted.

Confirmatory Factor Analysis. Confirmatory Factor Analysis (CFA) allows for the statistical testing of a hypothesized factor structure. With a scale such as the JSS, one would posit a structure where each item loads on its subscale. CFA would be used to indicate how well a set of data fits the hypothesized structure.

With exploratory factor analysis, the best fitting factor structure is fit to the data. With CFA, the structure is hypothesized in advance, and the data are fit to it. Factor loadings are estimated, just as they are in the exploratory method. In addition, CFA yields indicators of how well the data fit.

At present the best way to conduct a CFA is with one of the available covariance structure modeling programs. The two most popular and widely available are LISREL (Jöreskog and Sörbom, 1984) and EQS (Bentler, 1985). Comments below about CFA will be limited to the covariance structure modeling approach. Details can be found in a number of sources, including Long (1983).

To conduct a CFA, the number of factors, the factor or factors on which each item will load, and whether or not the factors are inter-correlated must all be specified in advance. Loadings on each factor for each item are represented in a loading matrix similar to that in explor-atory factor analysis, where items are represented by the rows of the matrix and factors are represented by the columns. Each element of the matrix is either set to a value of zero, meaning it does not load on the factor, or freed so that its loading can be estimated by the analysis. To conduct this analysis, you "free" the elements for each factor corre-sponding to its hypothesized items. All others are "fixed" equal to zero.

There is also a matrix representing the correlations among factors. These can be fixed to zero, making this an orthogonal or uncorrelated factor analysis. Alternately, they can be freed to allow the program to calculate the correlation among factors.

The logic behind freeing and fixing is that one fixes those correla-tions (or loadings) that are hypothesized to be equal to zero in the pop-ulation. One frees the correlations (or loadings) that are expected to be greater than zero (in absolute magnitude). There are two ways in which this "model specification" can be wrong: a fixed loading might actually be nonzero, or a freed loading might be equal to zero. If the factor struc-ture is properly specified, both in terms of the number of factors and the pattern of fixed and free parameters, the data should fit well. Of course, good fit of the data to the specified model may not be achieved because of sampling error, particularly with small samples.

The CFA analysis will yield estimates of the factor loadings and interfactor correlations. It also will give significance indicators (T val-ues in LISREL) for each free parameter. All freed parameters are ex-pected to be relatively large and significant. The analysis also gives several indicators of overall fit of the data to the model.

Both overall fit and individual parameters should be inspected to reach a conclusion about how well the subscale structure holds up. It is possible for some subscales to hold up well, while others do not. This occurred with the exploratory factor analysis of the JSS. It is also pos-sible for the overall structure to yield good fit indices, although many of the loadings are quite small and nonsignificant. In fact, incorrectly freeing a parameter causes less effect on the overall fit than incor-rectly fixing one that should not be. This is because an incorrectly freed

TABLE 6.3
Summary of Correlations of Work Locus of
Control Scale (WLCS) with Criteria

Criterion	Number of Samples	Number of Respondents	Mean Correlation
General locus of control	3	800	.54
Job satisfaction	5	968	−.54
Organizational commitment	3	222	−.24
Intent to quit the job	5	667	.23
Work autonomy	2	579	−.13
Influence on decision making	3	220	−.37
Role stress	1	287	.32
Supervisor consideration	3	182	−.31
Supervisor initiating structure	2	133	−.33

parameter can be estimated to be its correct value of zero, but an incorrectly fixed parameter is set equal to a value of zero, which might be far from its real value.

A CFA that fits well indicates that the subscale structure may explain the data, but it does not mean that it actually does. That is, support for the subscales in an instrument is not very strong evidence that they reflect their intended constructs. Such conclusions must be based on additional evidence of the types discussed in this chapter.

Validation of the WLCS

Validation of the WLCS is illustrative of the approach typically taken by scale developers. The major validation evidence was provided by correlating scores on the WLCS with several criteria expected to relate to it. Factor analysis was used to explore the dimensionality of the scale.

Criterion-related validity data were provided by six studies in which they were used (summarized in Spector, 1988). These studies provided correlation coefficients between the WLCS and 10 criteria. In all but one case, each criterion was used in more than one study. Table 6.3 provides a summary of the criterion-related validity results. For each variable the number of samples, total sample size across all samples, and mean correlation is shown.

The first criterion with which the WLCS was expected to correlate was general locus of control. This was because work locus of control is a domain-specific aspect of general locus of control. In theory, individuals who are internal (or external) in general locus of control should have a tendency to score in the same direction in an individual domain. Because these two types of locus of control are assumed to be somewhat distinct, the correlation between their measures should be only moderate. That is, it should not approach the reliabilities of the scales. As can be seen in Table 6.3, the mean correlation across three samples was .54. Thus the WLCS relates well to general locus of control, but not so well as to raise questions about its discriminant validity.

The remaining criteria were chosen because they were expected to correlate with work locus of control. Based on reviews concerning general locus of control in the work setting (O'Brien, 1983; Spector, 1982), variables were chosen that were expected to correlate with work locus of control. Specifically, internals were expected to perceive more autonomy and influence at work, to have better job attitudes, to experience less role stress, and to report their supervisors to be higher on consideration and initiating structure. As can be seen, correlations were found for these variables in the direction expected. Overall, they support the validity of the WLCS.

One troublesome finding, however, is the low correlation between work locus of control and autonomy. Because autonomy is a control-related variable, one would expect internals to perceive more of it than externals. One might speculate about the reasons for this weak correlation (e.g., perhaps job autonomy is so clear-cut and unambiguous on the job that everyone sees it about the same). More research would have to be conducted to determine if the lack of strong support for this hypothesis is a problem for the validity of the scale or the hypothesis.

An exploratory factor analysis was conducted on the WLCS with data from the original developmental sample. Summarized here are the results from the final 16 items. Table 6.4 contains the eigenvalues, which reflect the relative proportion of variance accounted for by each factor. The final column of the table contains the actual proportions. As can be seen, a single factor does not account for even a third of the variance in these items. This suggests the need for additional factors.

When two factors were rotated, the results were rather interesting. Table 6.5 contains the loadings for each item on the two factors. Included also is direction of the item wording. The italicized values represent the

TABLE 6.4

Eigenvalues for the 16-Item Factor Analysis of the Work Locus of
Control Scale (WLCS)

Factor Number	Eigenvalue	Proportion of Variance
1	5.08	31.8
2	2.27	14.2
3	1.21	7.6
4	.97	6.0
5	.86	5.4
6	.79	5.0
7	.73	4.6
8	.69	4.3
9	.63	4.0
10	.54	3.4
11	.46	2.9
12	.44	2.7
13	.42	2.6
14	.35	2.2
15	.30	1.9
16	.25	1.6

factor on which each item loads best. This factor structure is very clear-cut, in that the external items formed the first factor and the internal items formed the second factor.

Separate internal and external subscale scores were calculated by summing only internally or externally worded items, respectively. Their correlation in the original developmental sample was −.32. This correlation, along with the factor analytic results, suggest quite strongly that work locus of control is comprised of two somewhat independent components—internality and externality. Several locus of control researchers have reached this conclusion for general locus of control, based also on factor analytic results.

As discussed above, however, factor analytic results are insufficient to conclude that factors represent independent constructs. Additional data are required to validate the separate components. Such additional data were collected for the WLCS. Separate internal and external subscales were correlated with criteria in two separate samples. In all, 32 pairs of correlations were calculated. Corresponding magnitude of correlations for the two subscales were statistically compared with *t* tests.

TABLE 6.5

Factor Loadings for Two-Factor Solution for the Work Locus of Control Scale (WLCS)

Item Number	Wording Direction	Factor 1	Factor 2
1	Internal	.02	.67
2	Internal	−.04	.59
3	Internal	−.16	.52
4	Internal	−.02	.52
5	External	.70	−.05
6	External	.73	−.13
7	Internal	−.02	.67
8	External	.74	.03
9	External	.78	−.15
10	External	.72	−.30
11	External	.70	−.08
12	Internal	−.14	.53
13	External	.77	−.14
14	External	.67	−.16
15	Internal	−.23	.65
16	Internal	−.27	.52

In only 1 of 32 cases were criterion-related validity coefficients different for the two scales. Had an adjustment been made for experimentwise error for multiple testings, the sensitivity to have found one significant difference would have been even less. The significant case was most likely caused by sampling error.

The convergence of results when both subscales were correlated with the same criteria suggests that only a single construct is represented in these data. However, this conclusion is not supported by the factor analytic results. There is one more piece of evidence that may help resolve this discrepancy.

Scores for both the internal and external subscales were graphed in a scatterplot. The graph showed restriction of range on both subscales. With an eight-item, six-choice scale, scores can range from 8 to 48. Internal scores ranged from only 26 to 48, and very few scores were below 30. External scores ranged from 8 to 37, with very few scores over 35. With this sample, few subjects scored high on externality. This restriction of range is probably responsible for attenuating the correlation between the subscales. It is expected that results would be different in a sample with more external subjects.

Validation data for the WLCS are promising at this time, but they are merely preliminary. Stronger validation evidence might be provided by using the scale with populations containing more strongly external individuals. Additional criterion-related validity studies also should be conducted. Finally, the possibility that the internal and external items reflect different constructs should be further explored, perhaps by continuing to investigate differential validity with other criteria.

Validation Strategy

Test validation requires a strategy that involves collecting as many different types of evidence as possible. An efficient strategy would be to begin validation at the beginning of scale development. The first administration of the initial item pool might include measures of additional criterion variables that can be used for validation. If the initial item pool results in a tentative version of the scale, data relevant for validation will be available. One then would test to see if the new scale relates to the additional criterion variables as hypothesized. If the sample is of sufficient size, factor analysis also could be done.

Assuming that the scale looks promising, additional validation studies would proceed. These might involve replication of earlier validity tests as well as new tests. As many different types of tests as possible should be conducted. One should not rely entirely on self-report questionnaires to validate a scale. Merely finding that the scale in question correlates with other scales given to the same person is not very strong evidence by itself. The evidence becomes much stronger if tied to convergent validities based on very different operationalizations.

As validation evidence begins to accumulate, it will become apparent that the scale seems to work as expected. At this point one can conclude that the test demonstrates construct validity. Bear in mind, however, that construct validity can be supported but it can never be proven. It is always possible, as with any scientific theory, that later work will reinterpret findings, rendering the original explanation incorrect. The nature of the construct assessed by the scale will be given a new interpretation. However, until that day comes, construct validity for the scale is assumed.

7. RELIABILITY AND NORMS

The last two things that must be addressed are establishment of reliability and compilation of norms on the instrument. Although they are being considered last, data relevant to both are collected during every administration of the scale.

Reliability has already been partially covered in the treatment of the item analysis. Part of the item analysis involved calculation of coefficient alpha and the establishment of internal-consistency reliability. Further effort should be exerted to replicate the internal consistency on other samples and to establish test-retest reliability.

It is also of interest to determine estimates of population values for means and standard deviations on scales. This information is useful in establishing the meaning of a score. The entire approach to normative testing is based on determining where individuals lie in relation to other members of their populations. A score is said to be high or low in relation to where the majority of the population scores.

Reliability

Internal-consistency reliability is an indicator of how well the individual items of a scale reflect a common, underlying construct. Coefficient alpha is the statistic most often used to assess internal consistency, although it is not the only statistic available. Even if a high level of internal consistency is achieved in the initial item analysis, it is a good idea to replicate it in subsequent samples. Availability of reliability estimates across different types of samples will expand the generalizability of the scale's reliability to a wider range of subject groups. It is a sound practice to calculate coefficient alpha every time a scale is used. There should be little variation in the magnitude of the statistic from sample to sample. There may be times, however, when a scale's internal consistency breaks down. For this reason it should always be checked. Calculating coefficient alpha is quite simple with a computer and appropriate statistical software.

Test-retest reliability should also be determined. This type of reliability reflects measurement consistency over time. It is literally how well a scale correlates with itself, across repeated administrations to the same respondents. An internally consistent scale often will have good test-retest reliability as well, but the degree of across-time consistency must be empirically demonstrated. Measures of stable constructs are expected to demonstrate high reliability over time, but exceptions can occur when the scale is designed to measure a construct that varies over time. Measures of a person's mood, such as happy or sad, are designed to assess how people feel at a specific moment in time. Because moods can change rather rapidly, test-retest reliability would probably be low unless the time interval was very short. Reliability data should be interpreted in light of the expected consistency of the underlying construct. For example, a scale designed to measure an enduring personality trait would be expected to demonstrate higher test-retest reliability than a scale designed to measure a more transitory mood.

For many scales, test-retest reliabilities have been calculated for varying time intervals. The longer the time period, the lower the reliability would be expected to be. An attitude should be quite reliable over a period of 1 or 2 weeks. It should be less reliable over a period of 20 years. Research on many constructs has shown impressive levels of reliability, even over spans of decades.

Test-retest reliability is quite easy to calculate. A scale is administered to a group of respondents twice. Names or some sort of unique, identifying code must accompany each respondent's scale. In this way the scores can be matched across the two administrations. A correlation coefficient would be calculated between the two administrations.

Reliability for the WLCS

The WLCS demonstrated an acceptable internal-consistency reliability coefficient of .85 in the initial development sample. Replication of internal consistency was necessary to be sure the items would continue to converge in other samples receiving only the final 16 items (rather than all 49). Furthermore, because the initial sample was comprised of students, it was essential to demonstrate internal consistency in samples of the employed persons for whom the scale was developed.

Coefficient alpha was computed in five additional samples, all of which were comprised of working people (see Spector, 1988). These samples represented a rather wide range of employees, including managerial and nonmanagerial levels, and public and private sectors. The heterogeneous nature of the samples allowed for greater generalizability of internal consistency across different groups of employees. Coefficient alpha ranged from .75 to .85 in these five samples, with a mean of .82. Internal consistency seems adequate and consistent across samples. It will continue to be monitored as the scale is used with other samples and in other circumstances.

There is only limited test-retest reliability data for the WLCS. One quite small sample of 31 college students took the WLCS on two occasions about 6 months apart. They were assessed during the final semester of their senior year in college, and again several months after graduating and beginning employment. The test-retest reliability coefficient was .70. This sample size is quite small and only gives a rough estimate of the test-retest reliability. Underway at the present time is a second study with a considerably larger sample of over 100.

Norms

In order to interpret the meaning of scores, it is helpful to know something about the distribution of scores in various populations. The scale of measurement for most constructs in the social sciences is arbitrary. The meaning of a score can only be determined in relation to some frame of reference. The normative approach, which forms the basis of much social science measurement, uses the *distribution* of scores as that frame of reference. Hence, the score for an individual is compared to the distribution of scores. The score is considered high if it is greater than most of the distribution, and it is considered low if it is smaller than most of the distribution.

In order to determine the nature of the population distribution, it is necessary to administer a scale to a large, representative sample. To generalize to the U.S. population, the entire population should be representatively sampled. Unfortunately, few social scientists have easy access to the general population. Most scales are developed and normed on more limited populations. The vast majority of scales are normed on college students. For some constructs, the college population may represent the general population quite well. For others the representation may be very poor. Unfortunately, it is difficult to know in advance how representative college students may be. This presents a problem for generalization beyond the actual population sampled.

To compile norms, one would collect data with the instrument on as many respondents as possible. Of course, reliability and validity studies will provide data that can be added to the norms of the instrument.

A thorough series of such studies should provide a good starting point for norm development.

To compile norms, one would calculate descriptive statistics across all respondents. The mean and standard deviation are the main statistics of interest. The shape of the distribution, including skewness and possible restriction of range, also should be examined.

If norms are combined across samples, one should be careful that the distributions are similar. This is of particular concern if the samples are different in nature. Data from several samples of college students with the same major from the same university over a rather limited time period could reasonably be combined. Data from college and noncollege samples, with different proportions of men and women, or from various ethnic groups should be combined with greater care.

This raises the issue of subpopulation norms. Some subpopulations (e.g., men versus women, whites versus nonwhites) may differ on some scales. These differences are usually of interest, and authors of many scales compile norms for various subpopulations. Gender and race are two obvious variables upon which populations can be divided. Others may be suggested by the nature of the construct of interest. One should be careful to investigate subpopulations that seem likely to differ. Of course, it would be impossible to study all possible subpopulations.

A serious scale developer will compile norms from as many diverse groups as possible. Crowne and Marlowe (1964) provided norms on their SD scale for several different samples, including college students, job applicants, and prison inmates. They broke down several of these groups further into males and females. The availability of normative data on different groups increases the likelihood that meaningful comparisons can be made.

Even if subpopulations exist, one might still wish to determine the overall norms for the population. To accomplish this, one must be careful that the sample is representative of the population of interest. For the major subpopulations, the sample should contain the same proportions as the total population. For the general population, for example, the proportion of males and females should be approximately equal, with perhaps slightly more females than males. If the population is high-level corporate executives, a representative sample would be comprised almost entirely of men. Of course, if there are gender differences in executives, male and female data should be used to generate separate norms.

Norms for the WLCS

Norms available for the WLCS were provided by data from seven samples, totaling 1,360 respondents. Six of these samples were those that provided the above-mentioned reliability and validity data. The seventh was a sample of 195 college students. The mean on the instrument was 38.1, with a standard deviation of 9.4. Note that the possible range on the instrument is 16 to 96, with a middle score of 56. This puts the mean for the instrument at 1.9 standard deviations below the middle of the scale. In other words, very few respondents from the populations sampled actually score at the external end of the scale.

The range-restriction problem encountered with the WLCS may well have been produced by the rather narrow populations sampled. Most of the respondents to the scale have been either college students or white-collar employees. It is possible that a broader sample of respondents would find more high externals.

Separate norms are not available for subgroups. There were no differences in the available samples between college students and full-time employed people. Future efforts should be directed at determining if other subgroups differ in their scores. It is of particular interest to locate populations in which respondents score in a more external direction. The restriction of range in scores from the available samples adversely affects the testing of hypotheses with the scale. One cannot compare internal with external respondents if there are no externals in a sample.

8. CONCLUDING REMARKS

The development of a scale is an ongoing process that really never ends. To a great extent, this is because most constructs are theoretical abstractions embedded in theoretical frameworks. The viability of a construct is tied to the viability of the theory in which it exists. Just as with theory, one can never prove that a scale actually measures the construct of interest. It can be demonstrated, however, that a scale behaves in a manner that is consistent with its theoretical framework. This makes the scale and its construct useful for both the social science researcher and practitioner. It must be recognized that future research may disprove the theory and the construct validity of the scale.

70

An important issue is determining when a newly developed scale is ready for use. There are no hard and fast rules to determine this, and often necessity presses a person to use a scale quite early in its development. At the least, an item analysis should be conducted and an acceptable coefficient alpha should be achieved before the scale is used for any purpose. Furthermore, it is strongly recommended that at least some validation data be collected before the scale is used. Reliability alone does not guarantee validity. Ideally, several types of validity data would be collected. Early uses should be considered to have two purposes, one being a validity study.

This monograph has covered all the steps necessary for developing a summated rating scale. As mentioned earlier, it is not recommended that an inexperienced person try to "cookbook" scale development by merely following the steps outlined here. Although this monograph has covered the steps, the treatment of many topics has been quite brief. Other sources should be consulted on the topics discussed here, including test theory, reliability, validity, and factor analysis. (Several references were suggested earlier.) For a first attempt, assistance should be sought from a person already skilled in scale development. With a more detailed understanding of these topics and some assistance, scales can be successfully developed.

NOTES

1. *Psychophysics* is the study of relations between physical stimuli and perceptions of those stimuli. The psychophysics concept of the threshold is defined as the intensity of a stimulus that is on the border between being strong enough to be perceived and too weak to be perceived by a person. It is operationalized as that intensity of stimulus that a person will report perceiving correctly half the time.

2. I wish to thank Michael T. Brannick for relating this story about the perils of factor analysis overinterpretation.

REFERENCES

ALLEN, M. J., and YEN, W. M. (1979) Introduction to Measurement Theory. Monterey, CA: Brooks/Cole.

BAGOZZI, R. P., and YI, Y. (1990) "Assessing method variance in multitrait-multimethod matrices: The case of self-reported affect and perceptions at work." Journal of Applied Psychology, 75: 547-560.

BENTLER, P. M. (1985) Theory and Implementation of EQS, a Structural Equations Program. Los Angeles: BMDP Statistical Software, Inc.

BRANNICK, M. T., and SPECTOR, P. E. (1990) "Estimation problems in the block-diagonal model of the multitrait-multimethod matrix." Applied Psychological Measurement, 14: 325-339.

CAMPBELL, D. T., and FISKE, D. W. (1959) "Convergent and discriminant validation by the multitrait-multimethod matrix." Psychological Bulletin, 56: 81-105.

CARMINES, E. G., and ZELLER, R. A. (1979) Reliability and Validity Assessment. Sage University Paper Series on Quantitative Applications in the Social Sciences, 07-017. Beverly Hills, CA: Sage.

CRONBACH, L. J. (1951) "Coefficient alpha and the internal structure of tests." Psychometrika, 16: 297-334.

CROWNE, D. P., and MARLOWE, D. (1964) The Approval Motive. New York: John Wiley.

EBEL, R. L. (1969) "Expected reliability as a function of choices per item." Educational and Psychological Measurement, 29: 565-570.

GUILFORD, J. P. (1954) Psychometric Methods. New York: McGraw-Hill.

JÖRESKOG, K. G., and SÖRBOM, D. (1984) LISREL VI: Analysis of Linear Structural Relationships by Maximum Likelihood, Instrumental Variables, and Least Squares Methods (3rd ed.). Mooresville, IN: Scientific Software.

KIM, J., and MUELLER, C. W. (1978a) Factor Analysis Statistical Methods and Practical Issues. Sage University Paper Series on Quantitative Applications in the Social Sciences, 07-014. Beverly Hills, CA: Sage.

KIM, J., and MUELLER, C. W. (1978b) Introduction to Factor Analysis. Sage University Paper Series on Quantitative Applications in the Social Sciences, 07-013. Beverly Hills, CA: Sage.

LIKERT, R. (1932) "A technique for the measurement of attitudes." Archives of Psychology, 22: No. 140.

LONG, J. S. (1983) Confirmatory Factor Analysis. Sage University Paper Series on Quantitative Applications in the Social Sciences, 07-033. Beverly Hills, CA: Sage.

MARSH, E. W. (1989) "Confirmatory factor analyses of multitrait-multimethod data: Many problems and a few solutions. Applied Psychological Measurement, 13: 335-361.

NEWSTEAD, S. E., and COLLIS, J. M. (1987) "Context and the interpretation of quantifiers of frequency." Ergonomics, 30: 1447-1462.

NICHOLLS, J. G., LICHT, B. G., and PEARL, R. A. (1982) "Some dangers of using personality questionnaires to study personality." Psychological Bulletin, 92: 572-580.

NUNNALLY, J. C. (1978) Psychometric Theory (2nd ed.). New York: McGraw-Hill.

O'BRIEN, G. E. (1983) "Locus of control, work, and retirement," in H. M. Lefcourt (ed.) Research in Locus of Control (vol. 3). New York: Academic Press.

PHARES, E. J. (1976) Locus of Control in Personality. Morristown, NJ: General Learning Press.

RORER, L. G. (1965) "The great response-style myth." Psychological Bulletin, 63: 129-156.

ROTTER, J. B. (1966) "Generalized expectancies for internal versus external control of reinforcement." Psychological Monographs, 80(1), Whole no. 609.

SCHMITT, N., and STULTS, D. M. (1986) "Methodology review: Analysis of multitrait-multimethod matrices. Applied Psychological Measurement, 10: 1-22.

SMITH, P. C., KENDALL, L. M., and HULIN, C. L. (1969) The Measurement of Satisfaction in Work and Retirement. Chicago: Rand McNally.

SPECTOR, P. E. (1976) "Choosing response categories for summated rating scales." Journal of Applied Psychology, 61: 374-375.

SPECTOR, P. E. (1980) "Ratings of equal and unequal response choice intervals." Journal of Social Psychology, 112: 115-119.

SPECTOR, P. E. (1982) "Behavior in organizations as a function of employee's locus of control. Psychological Bulletin, 91: 482-497.

SPECTOR, P. E. (1985) "Measurement of human service staff satisfaction: Development of the Job Satisfaction Survey." American Journal of Community Psychology, 13: 693-713.

SPECTOR, P. E. (1987) "Method variance as an artifact in self-reported affect and perceptions at work: Myth or significant problem?" Journal of Applied Psychology, 72: 438-443.

SPECTOR, P. E. (1988) "Development of the Work Locus of Control Scale." Journal of Occupational Psychology, 61: 335-340.

SPSS Inc. (1988) SPSS-X User's Guide (3rd ed.). Chicago: Author.

WIDAMAN, K. F. (1985) "Hierarchically nested covariance structure models for multitrait-multimethod data." Applied Psychological Measurement, 9: 1-26.

WOTHKE, W., and BROWNE, M. W. (1990) "The direct product model for the MTMM matrix parameterized as a second order factor analysis model." Psychometrika, 55: 255-262.

ABOUT THE AUTHOR

PAUL E. SPECTOR is Professor of Psychology in the psychology department at the University of South Florida, where he has been since 1982. His research interests include complex statistics, psychometrics, and human behavior in work settings. He has published in many journals, including *Psychological Bulletin, Journal of Applied Psychology,* and *Applied Psychological Measurement.* He wrote *Research Designs,* another monograph in the Sage Quantitative Applications in the Social Sciences series.